Praise

Wynter Pitts and the
Lena in the Spotlight Series

"Tween girls LOVE fiction, but it doesn't always teach them the best values. That's why I'm so excited about Wynter Evans Pitts writing with her daughter Alena. This is a book series that will entertain your daughter's love of reading, but also introduce godly living. Enjoy!"

—Dannah Gresh

"Alena Pitts is an absolute treasure! She and her parents have a heart for ministry and for advancing God's kingdom. One of the best decisions we made in casting for the movie *War Room* was in choosing Alena to be Danielle. She not only brought an outstanding performance to the film, but she and her family were a joy to work with. We can look forward to great things from this little world changer."

—Stephen Kendrick

Every little girl dreams and Alena Pitts has written a delightful book series that will help any girl do just that. Taking a cue from her own life as a young actress, Alena weaves a story that will take her reader on a fun adventure while simultaneously encouraging her to both dream and keep first things first. The concepts of faith, family, and following your dreams are all laced together into a tale that is sure to keep any girl turning the pages while she also learns life lessons and is reminded of God's love.

—Chrystal Evans Hurst Co-author of *Kingdom Woman*

Day Dreams &
Movie Screens

Other Books by Lena Pitts with Wynter Pitts

Lena in the Spotlight Series

Hello Stars (Book One)

faithgirlz

LENA IN THE SPOTLIGHT

Day Dreams & Movie Screens

BY ALENA PITTS

WITH WYNTER PITTS

ZONDERkidz™

HarperCollins
PUBLISHERS
Since 1817

ZONDERKIDZ

Day Dreams and Movie Screens
Copyright © 2017 by Alena Pitts and Wynter Pitts
Illustrations © 2017 Zondervan

This title is also available as a Zondervan ebook.

Requests for information should be addressed to:
Zonderkidz, *3900 Sparks Dr. SE, Grand Rapids, Michigan 49546*

ISBN 978-0-310-76063-4

Cover Illustration: Annabelle Metayer
Interior Illustrations: Jacqui Davis
Interior design: Denise Froehlich

Printed in the United States of America

17 18 19 20 21 22 23 24 25 /LSC/ 15 14 13 12 11 10 9 8 7 6 5 4 3 2 1

Daddy, thank you for always encouraging
me to be my best and for teaching me
what it looks like to follow God always.
I love you.

Chapter 1

"Lena!" "Lena!" "Lena!"

The sudden chanting of my name caused my knees to jerk and the skin on my face to tighten. I peeked from underneath my shaggy green blanket just enough to see if the voices were as close as they sounded.

The room was empty but the repetitive squeals from my younger sisters, Ansley, Amber, and Ashton, let me know that they were close.

"I'm in here!" I spoke in a voice slightly above a whisper, desperately wanting to delay my discovery by just a few more seconds.

I was on the last page of the first chapter of my new book, *Winter Nights* by Mallory Winston. I had been waiting to read Mallory's book ever since I found a signed copy at the bottom of my green polka-dot travel bag three days ago. It was tucked right underneath my black and gold star-covered journal, on top of a baggy full of leftover chocolate chip cookies and an old slide from my last day of filming.

I ran my eyes across the last line of page twelve and quickly flipped the page. My sisters called my name once again, but this time they were standing near my head. The shrieking pitch of their voices practically pierced my ears. My whole body shook as they jumped up and down, pressing their hands into the cushions and bumping the game room couch.

"Lena!" Ansley knelt down and tucked her head right under the blanket with me. I reached up and pulled her completely down next to me and tickled her.

"Le—na—stop—Le . . . ha-ha-ha," she tried to speak through her giggles but I refused to let her.

"Huh? Stop laughing so much! I can't understand you!" I continued to tickle her for a few more seconds, then finally let her go so I could hear what she wanted so badly to say.

She sat up and tried to catch her breath. "Lena, Mommy wants you!"

"Oh, oops!" I said while pretending to reach for her one last time before I jumped up off the couch.

"Hurry up, Lena!" Ashton urged with a hint of excitement in her voice.

"What are you guys up to?" I asked, slightly suspicious. They seemed a little too excited and eager.

"Nothing," Amber blurted out.

I shook my head at their failed attempts to act normal and darted off in search of Mom.

I could hear the three of them following me down the hall, through the kitchen, and toward Mom and Dad's room.

When we reached my mother's room, Amber, Ashton, and Ansley stopped at the doorway and took two steps back.

Ansley balled her hands into tiny fists, tucking them under her chin with a huge grin.

"Mom?" I called as I peeked my head through the open door.

"I'm in here, Lena," she responded from behind her bathroom door. I slowly pushed the door open and spoke cautiously, "Yes, ma'am?"

There were bubbles teasing the edge of the big tub and the smell of peppermint tickled my nose.

My mother stood still. Her smile was bright. "Lena, this is for you." Her voice was soft and crisp at the same time as she waved her hand toward the bubble bath.

"Huh?" I asked.

My mother never let anyone, especially not one of us girls, near her bathtub. It's her favorite spot in the entire house.

She chuckled and said, "Yes, Lena, you heard me. Tonight this bath is for you."

I could hear my sisters giggling outside the door as Mom continued to speak, "I know this summer was not easy for you. You missed your friends and had to cancel a lot of your plans. You worked really hard in Los Angeles. I know you didn't have a lot of time to relax. So, before school starts tomorrow, I wanted to give you a chance to really relax. My bathtub is the most relaxing place in the house—at least in my opinion!"

She walked toward me, cupped my chin in the palm of her hand, and said, "I'm proud of you. Love ya. Now enjoy!"

She pulled the door closed behind her as I quickly got rid of my clothes. Then I practically dove in. The top layer of bubbles dispersed and splashes of water hit the floor.

"My book!" I gasped. I remembered I had left it in the game room and I really wanted to keep reading it.

"Ansley!" I yelled through the tiny crack in the door and prayed she could hear me. "Can you please get my book?"

A few seconds later, Ansley came dashing into the bathroom empty handed.

"What'd you say?"

"Ansley, I was asking you to bring me my book. Please!"

"Ohhhhh," her voice trailed off as she spun around on her heels and sped out of the bathroom, leaving the door wide open.

"SHUT THE D . . . Ahh, oh well," I murmured to myself.

I partially closed my eyes and waited. The smell of peppermint lingered and the water felt like warm silk.

I leaned my head against the tub. Just as my mind began to drift, I saw a flash of grey and white fur coming toward me.

"*No, Austin!*" I screamed as my grey bully pup burst through the open door and did a nosedive into the tub, right on top of me. The remaining bubbles dissolved and water splashed everywhere. Within seconds, Austin popped his soggy face up and placed his front two paws on the edge of the tub. He flung his floppy ears from side-to-side before jumping out. He gave his tail a dramatic shake as he trotted back through the door as if nothing had happened.

Mom's fluffy grey rug was so wet it had turned two shades darker. Splashes of water ran down the mirror above the sink and Austin's wet paw prints made a trail leading out the door.

I wasn't sure if I should jump out and attempt to fix Austin's mess or pretend not to notice and finish trying to relax.

Deciding it would be better to try to fix the mess, I stood up and reached for my towel. Of course, it was wet, so I grabbed another towel from Mom and Dad's linen closet, wrapped myself up tight, and used my own wet towel to clean up the floor.

I was on my knees swiping the wet towel over Austin's footprints when Mom walked into the room with the phone up to her ear.

She pursed her lips, but before she could ask me anything, I looked up and said, "Austin."

"Oh, okay. Well, Lena . . . , " Mom started to mouth words to me, but I couldn't make them out. She was holding her phone out with one hand and directing my attention to the phone with the other.

"Huh?" I mouthed back to her.

"Mallory," Mom mouthed to me and then started speaking out loud again. "I'll have Lena call you right back. Is that okay, Mallory?"

My eyes and mouth opened as big as they possibly could. "Mallory?" I gasped.

Mom said goodbye and pushed the button to end the call.

"Yes!" she laughed. "That was Mallory."

"What did she want?"

Mom's eyes widened with her huge grin.

"You'll see when you call her back." She beamed. "After we clean up this mess, of course!"

She shook her head and joined me on the floor.

With a little laugh, I begged her one last time to tell me what Mallory wanted, but she refused to break her silence. We wiped towels across the floor as fast as we could. I had not talked to Mallory since our last day of filming three weeks ago. My mind kept running in circles trying to figure out what she could possibly want to talk about.

As I stood up to gather the now dripping towels, Mom reached out and grabbed them from me.

"Do you want to finish your bath? It was supposed to be a relaxing treat for you before you start middle school tomorrow—sorry Austin ruined it."

"No way! I can't relax now. I need to call Mallory back! Can I FaceTime her?"

"Sure, just get dressed first."

Holding onto my towel tightly, I sped down the hall and into my room. I spotted the gray *Above the Waters* sweatshirt my director Mr. Fenway had given me on the last day of filming, threw it over my head, and slid into a pair of black leggings.

"Mom! I'm ready!" I yelled as I made my way back down the hall followed by Austin, Ansley, Ashton, and Amber.

Mom handed me her phone and said, "It's already ringing."

A huge smile was plastered across my face when Mallory appeared on the screen.

"Hi, Lena!" Mallory squealed with her usual enthusiasm.

In unison my sisters and I squealed back, "Hi!"

Even Austin yelped a little from all the excitement. Mallory had a way of bringing the excitement out in everyone.

I stared at her for a moment as she greeted each of my sisters individually. She looked so pretty as always. Her eyelids were covered in silver sparkles that matched her lips and her shirt. Of course, she was wearing her feather earrings and her hair was smoothed into a big bun that nestled just above her right ear.

"Well, I wanted to give you a call to check on you. I miss seeing you and your family every day! How's it going since you've been home? When does school start?"

"Aww, I miss seeing you too, and everyone from the cast and crew. I still can't believe I was in an actual movie. Feels fake—like it never really happened."

"Not *was*, Lena. You *are* in a real movie!" Mallory assured me playfully.

I smiled and continued, "School starts tomorrow. I am so excited to see my friends."

"Well, that's why I wanted to talk to you."

Mallory's expression changed slightly, and I could tell she wanted to tell me something important. I leaned in closer to the phone to make sure I didn't miss anything she was about to say.

"Lena, I think you know how proud of you I am. You worked really hard this summer, not just at memorizing your lines for the movie, but also at having a good attitude, even when it was really hard for you. You trusted God when you didn't understand everything He was doing, and you had fun in new circumstances even though you missed home and your friends a whole lot! Whether you realize it or not, you really showed us all what it means to trust God, and to grow. That's so important."

Mallory paused and I said the only two words that came to mind, "Thank you."

"Aw, you're welcome, sweetie. I meant everything I said!"

I was so close to the phone my nose was practically touching the screen.

"I'm heading out on tour to record my new live CD, and because *Above the Waters* will be in theaters in a few weeks, I want to do something special to help promote it. I plan on showing clips of the movie and sharing my experience with the audience at the opening of every show. Sooooo, I was wondering if you might want to come along! It would be so much fun, and I would love for people to see how God is using your talents as well!"

"Uhhh, wow." I could have kicked myself. I could not believe that was all I could think to say. But I could not believe my ears.

"Lena, I'm asking you to come on tour with me! I already talked to your mom and dad. You would have to miss a few weeks of school, and I know how excited you are to be back. Your mom thinks she can arrange it so you can take your schoolwork on the road with us, but it would mean leaving your friends again. Just for a little while though. The tour is only three weeks.

"I'm sure you need time to think it over. Will you pray about joining me and sharing your story?"

I was trying to process everything Mallory was saying. But my thoughts were bouncing around in my head, and I couldn't control them.

I looked up, and Mom was sitting at the kitchen table smiling from ear-to-ear. She nodded to let me know she approved.

"I can't believe it!" I finally had a few more words to say. "That would be so cool! So yes, I'll pray about!"

I watched as Mallory's expression relaxed a little. "Wonderful! And I can't wait to see you on the red carpet next month!"

"I can't wait to see you either. Maybe even before then."

"Can I pray for you now, before we hang up?" Mallory asked.

"Yes," I responded with a nod.

"Dear God, thank you for Lena. God, I know how much she loves you, and I am so grateful for the possibility of having her join me on tour. I pray that you would give her wisdom and let her know what it is that you want her to do. Thank you for her heart and for her love for you. Also, thank you for her family and her sisters, Ansley, Ashton, and Amber! Give them all a great night and wonderful first day of school tomorrow! Amen."

"Amen!" Ansley, Ashton, and Amber shouted. As soon as they heard their names mentioned in Mallory's prayer they had gathered back around the phone.

"Alright, girls, I'll talk to you all soon!" Mallory said.

"Goodnight, Mallory!" Mom called as we hung up the phone.

I could feel Mom staring at me as she waited for me to share my thoughts.

I looked up and smiled. "Wow, that's awesome that Mallory wants me to go on tour with her. But . . ." I hesitated, choosing my words carefully.

"I'm going to pray about it."

I could tell from Mom's continued stare that she was confused about my lack of excitement and wanted me to say more, but I didn't really know what else to say. So I smiled one last time and looked away. Singing with Mallory has been a dream of mine since before I even met her, but this didn't sound like I would be singing. I wasn't sure I wanted to talk to crowds of people, and I wasn't sure I wanted to miss so much school. This was my first year of middle school after all, and I was really looking forward to being with my friends again.

"Okay, girls, let's get ready for bed. As soon as Dad gets home, we will pray and go to sleep. Big day tomorrow for everyone!"

We all giggled and scurried off down the hall to get settled in for the night. A few moments later Dad was home. He prayed with us and tucked us each into our beds.

Thoughts of being on tour continued to fill my brain. I didn't know what I wanted to do, so I decided to make a list of pros and cons.

Hello, Stars,

It's me. It's been a while since we've talked, but things have been a little crazy around here. After we got back from California we took a little vacation to visit my grandmother in Colorado. Dad really wanted to drive but Mom convinced him to let us fly. I'm so glad we did because Colorado is really far from Dallas. Well, anyway, I am back home now and need your help. Things are getting weird again. Mallory wants me to go on tour with her. This is like a total dream come true! Except all I really want to do for a while is be normal, go to school, and hang out with my friends. So, here's what we need to do—make a list.

PROS OF GOING ON TOUR:

1. Hang out with Mallory
2. Visit many new cities
3. Live on a bus with Mallory
4. Make new friends
5. Make fun memories
6. Use the gifts God has given me
7. Skip school

CONS OF GOING ON TOUR:

1. Leave my friends again
2. Miss volleyball tryouts
3. Get behind in schoolwork
4. Leave my family
5. Sleep on a bus
6. Miss my friends . . . a lot

Can you help me, please? I want to make the right choice.

Chapter 2

"Are you awake?" Ashton's breathy whisper filled my ears.

My mouth popped open, my eyes stayed shut, and I blew the sound "shhhh," from my lips.

"But I can't sleep. I'm too excited!" Ashton replied.

I hesitated before opening my eyes and hoped that I was dreaming. As Ashton continued to talk, I realized this was not a dream. She was wide awake and wanted me to join her.

"Aren't you excited to start school, Lena?" she asked. "Were you excited when you started first grade? I wonder what my classroom will look like . . ." She went on and on.

I rolled over and squeezed my eyes shut tight before forcing them to open, desperately wanting to tell Ashton to go back to bed. But one look at the excitement in her bright brown eyes, and I could no longer hush or ignore her enthusiasm. Her hair was nestled on top of her head in a mix of bouncy curls and tangled coils. She had the same look of excitement as she did the night before Christmas, except it was September and there were no surprise presents waiting in the living room for us.

Her wiggling toes peeked through the bottom of her footless pajamas, and she flopped on my bed and folded her legs under her bottom.

"I wish I was in the sixth grade." She paused momentarily. "But first grade will be fun too, right, Lena? Will I have Mrs. Blount?"

I parted my lips just a little and smiled. In an effort to wake up, I raised my head but quickly dropped it back onto my pillow. "Ashton. What time is it?" I asked.

"I don't know," she answered and quickly picked up the conversation right where she'd left off. "So, Lena, will I have Ms. Blount? You didn't answer me. Did you have her when you were in my grade? She scares me. Just a little . . . Is she really scary?"

Her final question caused me to sit up. I smiled, let out a long breath of air, and then reached my arms up around her neck and pulled her into the bed beside me.

"Oh, Ashton! Don't be scared. You won't have Ms. Blount until fifth grade; anyway, she's not *that* bad!"

Ashton giggled and rolled to the right to rest her head against my chest. I patted her sandy colored curls down and wrapped my arms around her. I love snuggling with her. Mom says that out of us four sisters, we are the most alike, which means I always know just what to do to make her giggle or settle down.

We lay quiet for a few seconds. Ashton's eyes were still bright and awake and every few seconds I gave her a big squeeze.

I reached over her and, with half of my body dangling from the bed, scanned my floor for the little clock Ansley had given me that summer. I spotted it within arm's reach and dove for it.

"Urghhhh. Ashton, it's only 5:00! You have to stop

worrying so much and get some sleep. School is going to be awesome . . . but not if you're tired."

Ashton's voice had taken on a new tone. Her words were slow and raspy but she refused to keep quiet, "But Lena, one more thing. Are you excited to ride the school bus this year?"

Ashton's words caught me by surprise. I fumbled through my answer, "Yeah, mmm, well, a little."

Hearing Ashton say it reminded me that it was just a few hours away and the thought gave me little knots in my stomach. The same little knots I had when I sent in my video to enter Mallory Winston's contest. They showed up again when I was actually chosen to audition, and then again when Mr. Fenway called to tell me I'd gotten the part and would star along with Mallory in his new movie. Now, because of school and Mallory asking me to go on tour, it was *double*-knotted!

Ooohh, no, not the knots! I thought to myself. I shook my head from side to side and tried to refocus my thoughts on the seven-year-old bundle of questions lying next to me. Now, Ashton was lying flat on her back, smiling, and staring straight up into my face waiting for a truthful response.

"I'm a little scared too," I confessed. "But we still have to go back to sleep for awhile," I said sternly.

When I closed my eyes, I pictured Dad standing with his Bible in his hand and telling me not to worry. Repeating his words always made the knots start to go away, and I knew they would help both Ashton and me right now.

I smiled and said, "Remember what Philippians 4:6 says?"

Ashton frowned and said, "Don't worry?"

"Yup! That's it. Don't worry about anything, not even Mrs. Blount or the bus. Just pray!" I paused and added, "And sleep."

Ashton completely ignored everything I'd just said and asked, "Are Savannah and Emma going to ride the bus too? It won't be that scary if they ride it with you."

I sighed and sank deep into my pillow.

"I haven't talked to them, but I really hope so. If not, it will be like a brand-new adventure where I get to meet new people. I can do it." I tried to convince myself that it really would be okay.

"Now, Ashton, be quiet before you wake up Ansley. It's really time for more sleep."

I peeked over at the bed across from mine to make sure Ansley was still resting peacefully. Thankfully she was. She never worries about much, so starting fourth grade was probably no big deal for her.

"Was Amber still asleep when you got up?" I asked Ashton.

"Dunno."

"Well, go back to bed. You're going to be exhausted on your first day of first grade!"

The morning light was just beginning to creep in through the tiny crack between my polka-dot curtains and the window. Now that I was awake, there were so many thoughts swirling around in my head.

I thought about Ashton's questions and asked myself the same things and a few more. *What will sixth grade be like? Will my teachers be mean? How will my old friends treat me now that I'm in a movie? Will they think I'm a movie star? Will I make new friends? What will happen if I decide to go on tour?*

The questions continued to come, the knots in my stomach tightened, and I quickly realized I was not going to get much more sleep.

I lay there for a few more minutes staring at the spinning white ceiling fan before making the decision to get up and start my day a little earlier than everyone else. I rolled over, placed one foot on the floor, and jumped out of bed.

I tiptoed out of my room, down the hall, through the dark kitchen, and into the game room.

Surprisingly, when I stepped into the room, I saw Dad sitting in the big brown chair against the back wall. His head was leaned back and his Bible was resting on his lap. I wasn't sure if he was awake, so I continued to tiptoe a little closer to him.

"Lena?" he said without opening his eyes.

I stepped closer, scooted his Bible over a little, and plopped onto his lap. "How'd you know?" I asked him.

"Just a guess. Why are you awake?" He let out a lazy chuckle.

"Ashton woke me up because she couldn't sleep. Now I can't sleep and she's out cold." I tucked my head under his chin. Dad's prickly neck brushed against my forehead.

"It's almost time to get ready for school anyway," he said quietly.

"I know. I think that's why I can't sleep." I waited for Dad to respond but somehow I knew his silence meant keep talking.

"I keep thinking about starting a new school, not to mention riding the bus. And now the tour thing, urghhhh! And I keep wondering if people will treat me differently when they find out I'm in a movie. Do you think they will all know?"

"Well, they may not know right away, but once it's in theaters in a few weeks—I'm sure they will."

"I guess I'm a little scared about it all," I said.

"Oh, that's nothing to be scared about. It's exciting!" Dad tried to cheer me up.

Then he reached down and flipped through the Bible on his lap.

I stopped him. "I already know, Dad. God says not to worry."

He smiled.

I paused and chose my words carefully. I didn't want to hurt Dad's feelings, but I wanted to be honest. "But right now that's not helping." I was hoping he had something else he could tell me that would help in a different way.

He pulled the Bible a little closer to his face and read, "Philippians 4:6–7 says, 'Do not be anxious about anything, but in every situation, by prayer and petition, with thanksgiving, present your requests to God. And the peace of God, which transcends all understanding, will guard your hearts and your minds in Christ Jesus.'"

"I know, Daddy," I said, resting my head against his chest again. "It's just hard."

"Yup, believing God will handle everything is hard sometimes. But it takes practice. And do you know what the best part is?"

25

"Nope."

"You've already been working on it!"

I wasn't sure what Dad meant, but he sounded very happy about it. "Huh? I have?"

"Yes, Lena, you spent the entire summer doing something you didn't believe you could do. But God was with you and you did it. So don't worry, he will be with you in sixth grade too."

Dad pushed his head forward a little and nodded toward his Bible. "Maybe you should start trying to study your Bible a little each morning. Sometimes I get scared or nervous about things and spending time in the Bible always helps." He slouched a bit more in his seat and leaned his head back again.

Hmmm, maybe Dad was right. I knew that it was praying and talking to God that helped me this summer so I made sure I did that every day, but I'd never thought about reading the Bible. Well, except on Sundays during church or when Mom and Dad asked me to read scripture during our family devotional time.

I thought about this a little longer, staring at the open pages covered in a mix of green highlighter and black ink. Any white spaces along the edges were covered in his tiniest handwriting.

"Daddy, why do you write in your Bible?" I asked.

"Well, it helps to remind me what God has done in my life, and it helps me to think about what God is saying to me. I don't want to forget anything, ya know?" Dad closed his Bible with one hand and pulled it close to his chest.

Dad's voice was peaceful, but he sounded a little tired.

I didn't want to keep him awake, but I really wanted to know more about reading the Bible. And I wanted to know how I could get mine to look like his.

"Daddy," I whispered against his chest.

"Hmm?"

"I am going to try to start reading my Bible like you do, but I don't know how. And I don't know how to do all the writing you do."

"Well, Lena, how do you eat an elephant?" he asked.

I sat up quickly, stared at him, and squeaked, "I don't eat elephants, Daddy!"

Dad chuckled deeply, while I remained confused and waited for his explanation.

"Right. But if you did, you would have to eat it one little bit at a time! It's too big to eat any other way. It's the same with the Bible. You just have to start reading it in bite-sized pieces."

"Ohhhhhh . . ." I said, pretending to get it.

Dad continued, "You can start with one verse and you can even read the same verse over and over again if you want, until you feel like you really understand it in your heart. God taught you so much about himself and his love for you this summer. Just think of how much more he wants to show you."

Dad pulled me close and kissed my forehead. "Love you, Lena," he whispered. "Now let's see if we can get a little more sleep."

I closed my eyes and whispered, "Dear God, teach me how to eat an elephant."

We both chuckled.

"Daddy," I whispered. "I want to go on the tour."

"Then let's do it. We'll call Mallory tomorrow."

I breathed in and out a few times then rested quietly on Dad's lap.

Chapter 3

I'm not sure how long it was before we both started snoring, but I woke up with my right cheek smashed against Dad's white T-shirt.

Mom was standing over the top of us patting our shoulders.

"Time to get up, sleepyheads," she said softly.

Dad opened his mouth in a yawn so wide I could see his tonsils. He let out a loud and boisterous sound. I hopped to my feet, reached down, and touched my toes, then stood tall and stretched up as high as I could.

"Did you two sleep in here?" Mom asked.

"No, Ma'am." I responded, then thought for a moment. "Well, sort of. It's a long story."

"Okay." She shrugged her shoulders and smiled. "Well, come get some breakfast."

As I headed down the hall, Mom called out, "Lena, guess who emailed last night?"

"Who?" Dad and I both questioned.

"Mr. Fenway. He gave me the information for the *Above the Waters* red carpet event next month. The event will be right here in Dallas, and they want you to host it!"

"Whoa!" Dad said enthusiastically. "Is it during Mallory's tour?" he asked.

"Wait. Host it?" I questioned, not even sure what that meant.

"It's the week after the tour. And, well, Mr. Fenway asked if you would say a few words to open the event. He would also like you to introduce the rest of the cast before they show the movie!"

I listened, and the excitement in Mom's voice became contagious.

"Wow!" I said. "That's so cool. Are they sure they don't want Mallory to do it?"

"He said you!"

I turned and ran toward Mom, squeezed her shoulders, and squealed.

"So, do you want to do it? Is that a yes?" Mom laughed.

"Yes!" I squealed. "That will be so fun! I wonder what I'm supposed to wear on the red carpet?"

"We'll find something," Mom assured me.

I jumped up and down and let out a really loud giggle. When my sisters heard the commotion, they ran in with Austin galloping as fast as he could on his little paws, trying to keep up.

"Lena, what happened?" Ansley asked.

Amber and Ashton looked on, waiting for an answer, while Austin let out two quick yelps.

"Hey, boy!" I reached down and pulled him into my arms, then turned to the three sets of eyes staring at me. "Mr. Fenway emailed."

"Oh, what does he want now? Does he want me to be in his next movie?" Ansley wiggled her eyebrows up and down and chuckled.

We all laughed as Ansley began striking poses.

"Okay, girls, let's get ready. You can't be late on your first day of school!" Mom said while still chuckling.

I put Austin on the floor and moved toward my room.

"Lena," Mom called out. "So Dad says you've thought more about the tour? Dad and I think it's a really great opportunity but we don't want to you do it if you don't want to. We want you to know there is no pressure." Mom wrapped her arms around my neck and hugged me tight.

"I know. But right now I just want to get ready for school." I raced down the hall and went straight to my closet.

As I scanned my closet for my purple tank top, I tried to focus on my outfit for the day but kept thinking about being on tour with Mallory and what I would wear on the red carpet. I tried to stop grinning but I couldn't control it.

Pulling my shirt off the hanger, I reached for my pink fluffy skirt.

"Hello, everyone. My name is Lena—Lena Daniels. Welcome to my first movie, *Above the Waters*! But first, I want to sing a song for you."

I pulled an imaginary microphone close to my mouth and belted out my favorite Mallory Winston song, "Run Away with Me."

"Lena?" Amber's voice startled me. "Are you talking to yourself?" She laughed.

"Yup! I'm just so excited!"

Amber shook her head and focused her eyes on the clothes thrown across my shoulder. "Ooooo, that's a cute outfit!" she said and spun in little circles until she was out of my room.

I dressed as quickly as I could and found Mom in the kitchen making sandwiches for lunch.

"Eggs are on the stove," she said.

"Okay, thank you." I could tell that Mom was focused as she carefully laid pieces of cheese on top of four pieces of bread.

Dad whistled as he came down the hall and into the kitchen. His face looked happy and it made me smile. I watched quietly as he wrapped his arms around Mom and gave her a big squeeze.

"Ew," Ashton said when she came into the room. We all laughed. Dad grabbed a plate and joined us at the table.

"Lena, your bus will be here soon!" Mom glanced in my direction, encouraging me to eat quickly.

She did her happy dance, clapping three times and wiggling her hips. "Are you all ready, my middle schooler?"

"Yep!" I shouted.

Ansley, Amber, and Ashton hopped up after me, and we all began grabbing our lunch boxes and stuffing them with bags of chips and tiny boxes of juice from the pantry.

"Lena," Dad called after me. "You know you are going to need to change."

"Change what?" I asked.

"You can't wear that tank top to school without a shirt under it."

"Oh, yeah. He's right," Mom chimed in.

I took a deep breath and said, "I'm going to be late!"

"Do it quickly before the bus comes," Mom said calmly.

I raced to my room as fast as I could with Austin nipping at my ankles. Grabbing a white T-shirt from my drawer, I put it on under my tank and stood in front of the mirror. Something didn't look right. I turned to the left and back to the right.

"Jeans!" I screeched. I reached in the closet and grabbed a pair of the jeans Kay B gave me when we finished filming.

"Lena, hurry. It's time to pray," I heard Dad call down the hall.

I kicked off my purple Converse, slipped on my jeans, put my Converse back on, and raced down the hall to join my family circle for prayer.

Dad was telling my sisters about the early morning Bible reading and eating elephants discussion we'd had. They seemed just as amused and confused as I had, but I think eventually we all understood what he was trying to say.

"Just a little a day," he said. "We'll talk more about it at dinner. Let's pray,"

"Dear God, thank you for a new school year. I pray that you keep the girls safe and give them a great understanding of their schoolwork and an even greater love and understanding of You. In Jesus' name, amen."

Chapter 4

As soon as we dropped hands, the big yellow bus honked its horn. I grabbed my things, kissed Mom, Dad, and each of my sisters, and headed for the door.

Austin chased me, yelping, until I reached down, kissed his furry back, and told him I'd see him after school.

"Have a great first day, everyone!" I shouted and shut the door.

When I stepped onto the bus it was already full. I stood at the front next to the driver and froze as I heard the squeaky glass door close behind me.

I immediately spotted Emma. *Yes!* I thought to myself.

She was sitting toward the middle of the bus with her back facing the door. There were two girls facing her and they all appeared to be in the middle of a conversation. I called out her name and made my way to the empty seat next to her.

"Lena!" she shouted once I reached her. She clutched my shoulders and started bouncing the two of us up and down on the bus's dark brown leather seat.

I was so happy to see her bright and smiling face! The last time we had seen each other was in California when she and Savannah surprised me with a Mexican fiesta after that horrible day we had lost track of time.

She still had her summer tan and her hair was in two swinging French-braids.

"I am so glad to see you!" I squealed. "I was scared I would be alone."

"No way! I'll be on here every day! We have so much to talk about!" Emma responded dramatically. "I'm so glad to have my friends all back together . . . Wait . . . You know Savannah's birthday is next week, right?"

My eyes grew wide, and I felt a tiny lump in my throat. Emma did not actually wait for me to reply, and I was relieved. Not only had I forgotten about my best friend's birthday, I also needed to let her know that I wouldn't be here to celebrate.

"How long do you think it will take us to plan the best party ever? Three days? Four days?" Emma continued. "Next Friday? My house or yours? I can ask my mom."

"Uhhhh, I don't know." I paused.

"What? You think we need more time? You want it to be at your house? I'm totally cool with that."

"Oh, no. It's not that." I hesitated again. "It's just, well, I am not sure that I'll be here next week." I watched as Emma's smile started to disappear.

"What do you mean?"

"Well, Mallory FaceTimed me last night and . . ."

"And what? Tell me!" Emma interrupted me eagerly, a little smile starting to reappear.

"Well, she's going on tour, and she wants me to go with her," I said quickly.

"Whoa! Like to sing?" she asked.

"Well, no. Not to sing. She will sing. But she wants me to talk to the audience."

"Wow! Lena, that's so awesome!" Emma's reaction was encouraging.

"It is awesome. I just didn't want to miss everything here at home like I had to this summer."

"No worries, we just need to plan this party in like a day! We have to celebrate before you leave!"

Emma stretched her arms out and placed a hand on each of my shoulders. "And we will still be here when you get back."

A few minutes later we pulled up to the front of a huge red brick building—the middle school. The bus pulled in line right behind all of the other yellow busses and kids began jumping out of their seats and rushing through the big glass doors.

As we waited for our turn to get off, I looked at Emma and whispered out of the corner of my mouth, "Everyone looks so old."

"Yeah, middle-schoolers are big!" Emma basically shouted.

"Yeah, they are huge!" a voice from behind spoke directly into my ear.

Emma and I turned to see an unfamiliar face staring at us. She reached out her hand and said, "I'm Emma. Nice to meet ya. And this is Lena."

A soft smile crept across our new friend's face as she shook Emma's hand first and then mine. "I'm Joey."

Joey had the whitest teeth I had ever seen. They were the color of a brand-new piece of chalk. Along with her teeth, I noticed she was wearing a cute pair of blue-rimmed glasses, a knee-length jean skirt with two large pockets in the front, and a yellow and blue shirt.

"I like your socks," I said. Joey looked down at the

little anklets peeking from the top of her plain black shoes. "Thanks," she laughed.

I slapped my hand across my forehead and joined her in laughter. "I meant your shirt . . . and your skirt . . . well your whole outfit!"

"Thanks!"

"Do you know who your homeroom teacher is?" I asked as we stepped off the bus.

Joey pulled a crumpled piece of paper from the front pocket of her skirt. She glanced at it quickly. "Mr. Kelly!"

Emma and I chirped, "Us too!"

"Perfect." Joey clapped her hands together three times. "Can I hang out with you guys? I don't know anyone else here yet."

"Sure," Emma said as she led our new pack through the school doors.

We followed the crowd into school and tried to pretend we knew exactly what we were doing. I let out a sigh of relief when I heard a loud voice greet us at the door. "Sixth grade?" A short boy with red hair was standing behind a table covered with various pieces of colored paper.

We nodded, and he handed us a yellow sheet of paper while pointing to the right. "Follow the yellow walkway, and find your room number."

His instructions sounded easy enough. We followed his orders and found our designated floor pattern. We pushed our way through the crowd and headed to Room 176.

I scanned the halls for Savannah, but there was no sign of her anywhere.

Joey talked the entire time. She would pause at each

door to make sure we weren't there yet, but as soon as she read the numbers she picked right up where she left off. I liked her and could tell we would be friends.

"I just moved here, to Texas. My dad took a new job, and my mom, well, she didn't really want to come, but she agreed to come for a few months and give it a shot. I hope she likes it because I like it here already. She really liked it at home in Florida.

"I'm gonna miss my friends, but I'm glad I've met you already. I've never lived anywhere else but Florida before so it's a little scary." She paused. "Oh, here we are!"

Right before we walked through the oversized wooden door, Emma blurted out, "Lena lived in California. She survived without us for an entire summer."

"Oh, really?" Joey asked.

Emma continued, "Yup, she's in a movie with the singer Mallory Winston!"

I stood still, surprised by Emma's words and braced myself for Joey's reaction.

Joey opened her mouth wide and flung her head back. "That is so cool!!! I'm friends with a real-life movie star!" she shouted.

Emma raised her arms from the elbows up and alternated between jazz hands and closed fists in order to imitate flashing lights. She kept repeating the words "movie star."

I grabbed each of her closed fists and playfully pushed them back down to her sides.

"Urghh, stop it! I'm not a movie star," I grimaced.

"Ummm, yeah, you totally are a movie star and I want to tell everyone!" Joey continued to speak very loudly.

"Please, don't!" I felt my cheeks turn warm and a slight smile started to force its way across my lips.

Just then I heard the door for number 176 squeak open and a firm and familiar voice caught my attention.

"Good morning, ladies. Welcome to room 176."

I gasped and took two steps backwards.

"Ms. Blount?" I couldn't resist sounding like a question.

"Yes! Come in, girls, and take your seats."

Ms. Blount didn't seem as surprised to see us as we were to see her. She casually watched as Emma, Joey, and I cautiously made our way to our seats.

Savannah was sitting in the third row and waved vigorously as we neared her desk. She jumped up and wrapped her arms around Emma's neck and then mine.

"Why is Ms. Blount here?" I whispered in her ear. She giggled and shrugged.

Savannah's desk was all ready for the day. She had two well-sharpened pencils and an extra eraser resting in the little indent at the top of her desk. Her blue spiral notebook was sitting right under them, and her clear water bottle with a blue and yellow striped "S" were sitting in the middle.

We carefully slipped past her and took the three seats to her right.

Ms. Blount stepped out of the room to find the rest of her students.

"What happened to the bus?" Emma asked. "I thought you were riding it too?"

"I was too scared!" Savannah giggled nervously at her own words.

"Scared of what?" Joey stepped forward and joined the conversation.

"Hi—" Savannah said with a bit of uncertainty in her voice.

"Oh, Savannah! This is Joey—she's from Florida. Joey, this is Savannah."

They both smiled and waved a little.

Ms. Blount stepped back into the room and Savannah immediately focused her attention straight ahead.

"Welcome to middle school, everyone." Ms. Blount clasped her hands and began to pace around the room. "Some of you were expecting Mr. Kelly. He's no longer here at A.W. Some of you I know from elementary school, and some of you are brand-new faces.

"This is your homeroom, and I am Ms. Blount, your class advisor and your Texas History teacher."

Ms. Blount began to teach and did not stop until the bell rang letting us know it was time for a break.

When we heard the loud ringing, Emma widened her eyes and mouthed, "Let's get out of here!"

Chapter 5

We gathered our things and jumped out of our seats as fast as we could. But when we reached the door, Ms. Blount called my name. "Lena Daniels—"

I cringed, a hint of fear running up my back.

Emma mouthed, "Catch ya later," and I watched the three of them exit the room. I could feel my heart thumping as I stood in front of Ms. Blount waiting to hear what she wanted me to do next.

"I just wanted to say welcome back." She spoke without smiling, but somehow her words seemed friendly. "How was your summer?"

"It was good," I spoke cautiously.

"Did you enjoy making the movie? What's the title again . . . and when will it be in theaters?" she continued to probe with sincerity.

"Yes, ma'am. The premiere is October 15th. It's called *Above the Waters.*" I answered as quietly as I could, hoping that no one else could hear.

Unfortunately, as soon as the words were said, a tall girl with short, dark brown hair who was still gathering papers into her backpack ran over to me and grabbed my shoulders, screaming, "I knew it was you! I saw you on the commercial with Mallory Winston! That's so cool!"

Her excitement felt overwhelming, and I had no idea

how I should respond. She continued to stare at me, and I completely froze. "Can I have your autograph?" she asked.

I felt Ms. Blount's arm around my tightened shoulders. She squeezed me a bit while telling my new classmate how proud of me she was, but school wasn't the place for autographs.

The girl gave me one last, huge grin and ran off into the hallway shouting my name to her friends.

I let out of a sigh of relief as Ms. Blount let go of me and said, "I'm so glad to have you in my class again, Lena."

I shifted my eyes and tilted my head from one corner of the room to the other to make sure she was talking to me. A few students lingered in the back of the classroom, but I was the only close one, and she continued to focus on me. This was not the Ms. Blount that I remembered from fifth grade. I wondered why she was being so nice to me, but I knew it was best not to ask.

I gave her one last smile and said, "Thank you." Then I dashed out of her room as fast as I could.

There were people everywhere. I peeked up and down the halls until my eyes met Joey's. "We're over here, Lena!" she bellowed, wildly waving her arms.

As I made my way to my own pack of friends, I could hear gasping and whispers. I could feel eyes staring at the back of my head. I picked up speed and tried to clear a path. But the faster I walked, the more I noticed strangers were beginning to smile and wave at me.

Uh-oh. I thought. I tried to avoid eye contact, but it was getting harder to pretend I didn't know who they were looking at.

For the remainder of my three-second journey down the hall, I plastered an embarrassed grin on my face and walked twice as fast as I normally did.

When I finally reached Emma, Joey, and Savannah, I could feel the little knots taking over my stomach. No one was actually talking to me, but I knew that everyone was talking *about* me.

I tried to disappear into my circle of friends, but the tall girl with brown hair grabbed my arm and hauled me toward her screaming, "Hey, listen up everyone! I would like to make an announcement! In case you hadn't noticed, we have a movie star here at our school! This girl is in the movie *Above the Waters* with Mallory Winston! I saw her in a commercial this morning!"

The whispers around me turned into a combination of giggles, screams, and loud gasps. A few people simply gave me a thumbs up, while others ran toward me with pens in their hands asking me to autograph their arms, hands, and backpacks.

The already chaotic middle school hallway had turned into a complete zoo and I was the main attraction! I was trying to look as normal as possible, but on the inside, I was mortified. My heart was pounding so hard I was sure everyone could see it through my shirt.

Suddenly, I saw a flash of red hair breezing through the crowd, and I felt relieved as Ms. Blount began shooing everyone off to their next class. "Party's over, kids. Let's go. Let's go. Everyone keep moving."

She looked at the four of us and repeated the same words.

I gladly led the way down the hall and out the back door toward the big field with rusted soccer goals on each end. There were a few people running through the grass and some resting along the sidelines.

I slid down the red brick wall landing on a soft patch of grassy dirt. "I guess this is going to be my life." I raised my knees, plopped my arms across them, and dropped my head into the little space between my raised knees.

'What's the big deal, Lena?" Joey asked. "I think it's so cool that you are in a movie. If I was in a movie, I would tell everyone. Why are you being so weird about it?" Joey's voice was high, and she seemed surprised by my reaction to the scene that had just occurred. "Everyone is going to see that movie; it has Mallory Winston in it!"

"Yeah, I know. I was just really hoping it wouldn't be a big deal. Makes me feel weird, that's all," I said.

"Well, I think it's pretty cool and exciting. Everyone was pointing at you like you are a star, and you are! Stars make people smile," Emma added.

I raised my head, looked up, and smiled at her. "I don't mind making people smile, but it just feels weird to have people ask me to write my name on their arm."

The thought made us all chuckle.

"I'm in the movie, but I was really just hoping to be me at school. I don't even know if it's going to be possible, especially when I leave for the tour." As soon as the words slipped out of my mouth, I remembered I had not had a chance to tell Savannah yet.

"Wait, huh?" she asked.

"She's going on a real-life tour with Mallory Winston!" Emma and Joey both answered.

"Wow, Lena, that's great!" Savannah said as she slid down the wall beside me and leaned in close for a celebratory hug.

"Lena, you know you are still *you*, right? *Above the Waters* is just something great that you did, and now this tour is just another awesome thing! It's like God gave you a really special gift and everyone wants to celebrate with you!"

I hopped up on my feet. "I get it. I'm trying to see it that way too," I said, staring at the toes of my shoes.

We all stood for a few seconds, looking at each other and smiling.

Finally, Emma broke the silence, "All good now, everyone?" she asked. "'Cause I'm hungry!"

"Yeah, let's go eat," I said, with Emma pulling me into a skip toward the glass doors that led directly into the cafeteria.

We managed to make it from the door to the line with only a few friendly nods and waves. We ate quickly, sorted through our schedules, and went our separate ways to finish what was turning into the weirdest first day of school ever.

A fixed smile remained on my face for the rest of the day as I posed for pictures, waved to new friends, and signed various objects and arms. By the time the last bell rang I was exhausted and my cheeks hurt from smiling.

I was mentally and physically wiped out. "Missing school" was definitely a pro to going on tour with Mallory.

I practically fell through the back door at home, then

shuffled down the hall to my room and landed on top of my shaggy green blanket. Austin chased after me searching for a greeting. He laid his squishy body next to me and scooted in close until the soft space between his forehead and nose was snuggled perfectly under my right arm.

My eyes closed, and I drifted off. The next sound I heard was Dad's voice calling me to dinner.

At dinner, the whole family discussed the details of the tour.

"Mom and I have talked about how to make it work so that we can all be a part of it. It will be hard for us all to be there the entire time. However, Mom will be with you for the whole tour, and the rest of us will fly to meet you for a weekend, or maybe even one of the three weeks," Dad said.

Mom nodded and chimed in to tell us that there would be two busses on the tour. One for Mallory and her band and the other just for our family.

Ashton, Amber, and Ansley's eyes lit up when Mom pulled up a picture of the bus on her phone.

"This will be so fun!" we all squealed.

That night, when I was sure everyone was asleep, I climbed out of bed, grabbed my Bible, and tiptoed across the shaggy turquoise rug. I quietly closed the bedroom door behind me and headed to the game room.

Just as I suspected, Dad was in there. The TV was turned up loud, but somehow Dad heard me coming and whispered, "Lena?"

"Yes, it's me," I answered. "I wanted to read my Bible tonight."

"That's great, Lena, but isn't it a little late?"

I looked down at my Bible, then back at Dad.

"Alright," he said, looking at me with that just-this-once expression. "I was telling Mom that I want to get you a devotional to help you get started with your Bible reading." Dad paused. "We just have to find one that's just right for girls your age. Then you can take it on tour with you and use it as a guide for what part of the Bible you're reading. You don't *need* to have one but it may be helpful."

I giggled, "A devotional to take on tour with me . . ."

Dad laughed and shook his head.

"Okay, Lena, I'm going to bed. Take a little time to read a verse or two then you should get some sleep too." I watched as he got up from his chair and slowly walked toward his bedroom.

After Dad left, I turned off the TV. The house was completely quiet and dark. As I looked around the empty game room, I whispered, "Thank you, God." Today hadn't been a perfect day, but it had been a good one.

I jumped up into Dad's big chair and sank down into the permanent indent made by his body. I flipped open my Bible and fumbled through the pages. Nothing seemed to make sense.

Just like eating an elephant, Lena, I told myself.

I flipped to the table of contents and read off the books of the Bible in my head. When I saw the book of Mark on the list, I paused. I remembered Mr. Fenway reading some of that to us this summer, so I decided it was probably a good place to eat tonight.

I skimmed the pages until I reached Mark 10:28. The words, "Peter began to say to Him, Behold, we have left everything and followed You," caught my eye. I read it several times.

"Peter left everything to follow God?" I whispered. I knew that Peter had crazy faith because he walked on water, but I never even thought about the rest of his life.

I read the verse one last time and leaned my head back against the chair like I'd seen Dad do. It kind of felt like that's what God wanted me to do by going on tour with Mallory. To follow Him.

I felt my eyelids getting heavy, so I pulled myself up in Dad's chair and grabbed my journal.

Well, God,

I think I am talking to You tonight. I really like Peter. Mallory reminds me of him. They both have crazy faith and do what You ask them to do. Will You help me to be like them too? I want to follow You everywhere! So many things happened today and I know it's because You planned it that way. So I guess I just want to say thank you! And God? Will You help me share my story without being scared? I want to be brave for You!

Chapter 6

I spent my first week of middle school trying not to be noticed as the girl in the movie, while planning to leave on a tour like some sort of celebrity. It felt weird, but with the help of my family and friends I survived.

Savannah forgave me for not being able to help plan her big birthday celebration, but we promised to celebrate together as soon as I got back.

And then it was finally Saturday morning—tour day—and it was time to go! Mallory's tour bus was meeting us an hour away from home, so I knew we needed to get an early start.

As I skipped down the hall, I could feel my heart racing with excitement. I burst into the chorus of my favorite Mallory song and within seconds, I was joined by Ansley, Ashton, and Amber. We danced and sang our way through our closets, in and out of the bathroom, and around the kitchen. Mom calmed us down so we could pray and discuss the final details of the day.

"Girls! Shhhh. Listen up. We have something to tell you."

Once Dad had our attention, he started talking. "So, everyone knows that Lena will be going on tour with Mallory today, right?"

"Yesssss!"

Mom continued talking, "Well, guess what?"

"What is it, Mommy?" Ansley could not take the suspense.

"Grammy is coming to stay here for a while! She is going to help while I am away with Lena!" Everyone gasped with excitement.

Grammy is my mother's mom. She lives in Colorado. We don't get to see her often, but when we do, we all love it! But hearing the news actually made me feel a little sad. If Grammy was coming to be with my sisters while I was on tour, then that meant I would not get to spend time with her.

I forced a smile and watched while everyone celebrated. Mom noticed the change in my enthusiasm and added, "And Lena, the best part is she will stay for a few extra weeks when the tour is over!"

I felt my eyes start to water and my mouth flew open. "Yes!" I screamed. I hopped up and down stomping my feet against the hardwood floors.

"Lena, are those happy tears?" Amber asked.

"And your happy dance?" Ansley added.

"Yup!" I replied. "Really happy tears and my happiest happy dance!"

I let out a final yelp and stomp and wiped some of the happy off my face.

"Girls," Dad started, "remember, God promises to take care of us! Grammy being able to come is an answer to our prayers! It will really help make this new adventure even more fun!"

Dad slid his Bible off the counter and read, "Philippians 4:19 says, 'And my God will supply all your needs according to His riches in glory in Christ Jesus.'"

"Daddy, so God's gonna make us rich?"

"No, Ashton," Daddy grinned. "It means that we don't have to worry about anything in our lives because God will take care of us. I was starting to worry about how we could let Lena go on tour but still keep our family together and even enjoy the opportunity as a family. Then last night, when I was reading my Bible, God reminded me of this verse. He will take care of everything because God supplies for all of our needs."

Mom leaned over and reached her arm around Dad's waist. She laid her head on his arm and smiled. "God loves us so much," she said.

"Awww, Mommy." Amber was all starry eyed as she watched Mom and Dad snuggle.

"Ew," Ashton mumbled before asking if she could pray.

"Yes, Ashton, go ahead." Dad gave her a nod and closed his eyes.

"Dear God, thanks for today. Thank you that Lena gets to go on tour with Mallory and that Grammy gets to be with us. Keep us all safe and help Lena not to miss us too much."

We all said, "Amen!"

"Let's load the car, everyone. Lena, do you have all of the notebooks and schoolwork you will need while you are gone?" Dad asked as he grabbed my luggage and headed to the van.

"Yes," I nodded. "I have everything I need."

"And Ms. Blount emailed me the websites and other information we will need to use to help her stay on track with her classes," Mom added.

While we were discussing my schoolwork, Austin slipped through the door and ran straight to the van. He hopped through the open door and took a spot on top of Ansley's lap.

"Oh, Austin!" Mom called.

"Can he ride with us?" I begged. Mom and Dad agreed.

Having Austin with us made the ride go quickly. He jumped from one lap to the other, licking and sniffing each of us until we arrived at a big empty parking lot.

"We're here!" Dad called from the driver's seat.

"Hey, Daddy—" I stopped mid-sentence as two huge, shiny black busses slowly pulled into the parking lot too and stopped right next to us. One of them had "Mallory Winston" painted in silver letters across the entire side.

"Mallory!" we all screamed.

We jumped out of the van and waited for Mallory to step off her bus. She looked comfortable in her baggy purple sweatpants and white hooded pullover, with the words "God's Girl" scribbled across the front. She was also wearing black high top Converse and a black baseball cap that hid most of her hair.

I let out a shriek as Mallory ran over to me. She hugged me as hard she could and we both started bouncing up and down. She gave me one more squeeze before letting go and letting out a long breath.

"Ahhh, Lena! It's so good to see you!"

After she hugged me, she grabbed each of my sisters and gave them each a big squeeze too. "Hi, girls! Seeing you all reminds me so much of my own family." She smiled at each of us and continued, "I'm the oldest too, Lena. That's part of the reason I chose you for the audition, originally. When I watched your video and listened to you tell about these kiddos, I loved hearing about the relationship you have with your sisters! Remember to never let anything come between you."

I held Mallory's words close and wrapped my arms around Ashton, Ansley, and Amber's necks.

We stood in the empty parking lot for a little longer. Mom, Dad, and Mallory discussed some of the details of the tour. They talked about the different cities, the churches we would visit, and the days Dad and my sisters would join us.

While they talked we girls chased Austin in circles.

When it was finally time for Mom and me to get on the bus, we held hands and Dad prepared to read from the Bible on his phone before praying. Ashton and Ansley couldn't stop giggling at Austin's failed attempts to catch his tail. Mom reached down and scooped him up before Dad started.

"Finally, brethren, whatever is true, whatever is honorable, whatever is right, whatever is pure, whatever is lovely, whatever is of good repute if there is any excellence and if anything is worthy of praise, dwell on these things."

With Austin squirming in her arms and nibbling on her pointer finger, Mom tried to remain calm and focused. Dad kept reading, "The things you have learned and received and heard and seen in me, practice these things, and the God of peace will be with you."

"Does anyone know what scripture this is?" Mom asked.

"Flipenny," Amber yelled while trying not to let her tongue get caught in the huge gap where her front teeth used to be.

Mom nodded, pushed Austin's paw away from her mouth, and smiled. "That's right, Amber, Philippians chapter 4, verses 8–9."

Dad reached out and gestured for us to come in closer. "Girls, and you too Mallory," he smiled. "Remember that you will hear and be tempted to think about a lot of things on the road, in school, and all around you. Someone may be talking about another kid on the playground, or you may be afraid of a decision you have to make, a song you have to perform, or even annoyed by something your sister is doing . . . but remember that God tells us to focus on good things in our day, the things that point us to Him. Try to look for God in your day today and always! Let's pray."

We closed our eyes, and Dad prayed that God would keep us all safe and use our gifts to bless others. When he finished, we exchanged long hugs and said, "See ya in a week!"

Mallory turned to Mom and me and said, "Okay, I'll let you guys get settled on your bus. We have to pick up two of my band members from the airport, and then we will head straight to our first show! Get a little rest. It will be a long night."

Mallory darted toward her bus, and I darted toward the other. I anxiously placed one of my purple Converse onto the first sparkly black step and then the next. I wanted to race up the remaining two steps, but the sound of my mother's voice stopped me.

"Lena, wait!" she was yelling.

My feet froze as I twisted from the waist up, held myself up with one arm on the huge open door, and leaned outside to see why my mother was calling for me. I hadn't even realized she wasn't with me anymore.

She was flailing her arms in the air and trotting toward me.

"Smile!" she said while laughing and pointing her phone at my face.

"Wai . . ." I tried to stop her.

"Got it. Okay, let's go," she said while playfully shooing me up the stairs and onto the bus.

I could not believe my eyes when I finally reached the top. This was not a bus at all. It was a fantastic, shiny new house on wheels.

The first thing I noticed was the huge television screen hanging from the wall behind the driver's seat. The words "MALLORY WINSTON" were in bold white letters just above the shiny black screen. There was music coming from the ceiling and everything seemed to sparkle.

"Whoa," I mouthed to my mother, without making a sound.

I stepped forward just enough for her to reach the top next to me. We both continued to stand and stare. The windows were outlined with tiny lights and there was a long dark brown leather couch on both sides of the bus. At the end of the couch on the right was a little table resting between two benches. It reminded me of our school lunch tables, except it was clean and new.

Directly across from the table was a countertop, sink, and black refrigerator. The outside of the refrigerator was so clean I could see the little table reflected in it.

Mom stepped in front me and strolled down the wooden floor between the two couches. She slowly turned her head from the right to the left, and then to the right again. When she reached the countertop, she rubbed her hand along the smooth surface and smiled. "Granite," she said.

"Huh?"

"The countertops. They're granite," she responded without looking at me. "Never mind . . . it's just a nice stone." She continued to stroll toward the back of the bus. "This is all so lovely."

I picked up a little speed and followed her though a small doorway covered by a long, gray curtain. On the other side of the curtain, the wide wooden floor became a narrow carpeted area. There were no more windows, just walls covered with more curtains.

"Ummmm," I said curiously as I stood in the little dark space.

"Beds," Mom said.

We took another few steps forward and walked through another doorway. The sunlight from two large windows greeted us again, and I heard Mom say, "Wow!" before I could actually see anything.

"What? What?" I tried to squeeze in front of her.

She walked forward a tad more, and I could not believe my eyes. We were standing in a big, beautiful bedroom. There was a slightly smaller TV screen hanging on the wall in front of a large bed covered with tons of pillows.

"I'm sleeping in here!" I squealed jokingly. I ran forward past Mom and dove onto the bed in the middle of all the pillows.

Mom smiled, but continued to look around and examine her new living space. It was very clear that this would be Mom and Dad's room when the family was all together on the tour bus.

"Lena," she laughed, "you can choose one of those beds out there behind the little curtains."

After inspecting the space a little bit more we went out to the living area of our temporary new home, ready to start this new adventure.

Mom and I sat on the long couches in front of the bus as we bounced up and down the highway. I watched from the windows as we stopped in another empty parking lot near the airport. While we waited for two girls to load their things on Mallory's bus, our door opened and Mallory called out our names before dashing up the stairs.

"So, what do you guys think of the bus? Can you live here for a few weeks?" she asked.

I could not help but smile. "Absolutely!" I yelped.

"Mallory, this is so great!" Mom stood up and reached one arm around Mallory's shoulder. "Thank you," she said.

"Aww, yay! I am so glad you like it." I could tell from Mallory's cheeky grin that she was just as happy as we were to start this adventure. "There should be plenty of space on here for your sisters too," she added then looked right at me.

"So, Lena, are you ready for tonight?"

"I am!" I said the words, and I meant them in my heart.

I didn't really know what I was ready for, but I knew that whatever it was, it was going to be fun.

"Okay, we are running a little behind, so we are going to head to the church now. When we get there, I'll have everyone in the band and crew introduce themselves, and I'll make sure everyone knows exactly what to do. Sound good?"

"Yep," I nodded.

Before Mallory left the bus, she walked up to the man sitting in the driver's seat of our new home on wheels and patted his shoulder. She grinned apologetically and said to us, "You know what? I think I forgot to introduce you to someone very special! This here is Mr. Ernie and he is your driver for the tour. Mr. Ernie is an expert driver and is going to take such good care of you and the rest of the family when they join us."

Mr. Ernie smiled gently and gave a wiggly finger wave at Mom and me before he started the bus up. He glanced back at us through his big mirror and nodded his head, letting us know we really were in good hands and Mom and I smiled back.

"It's nice to meet you, Mr. Ernie," we both said, as we watched Mallory hop down the steps and jog back to her bus.

Mallory had told us we were close to our next destination, so I decided to use my time to write Savannah a quick, special birthday note. I wanted her to know that I would be thinking of her on her special day. I went to grab some notepaper and jotted a note to my best friend.

Dear Savannah,

I wish you could be here with me. The bus is so cool and it would be the perfect place to have a birthday party. I already miss you and Emma and Joey! I know I am doing what God wants me to do, and I want to thank you for helping me see that! Thank you for being the best friend ever!

Love, Lena

Chapter 7

We pulled up to a white church on a busy road with a sign outside that read, "Welcome Mallory Winston and Lena Daniels!"

"Mommy, look!" I shouted. Mom stood up and leaned close to the window for a better look.

"Wow! That's wonderful!" she said.

When the bus stopped moving, I could see a group of five people standing in a jumbled circle right outside the church doors. They were all wearing black jeans, dark shirts, and black shoes, which seemed like a sort of uniform for them, and were looking at stacks of boxes scattered around the area.

The tallest guy in the group turned and began waving eagerly when he saw us through the large glass window.

I waved back and watched as he reached down and grabbed a clipboard off one of the boxes and wandered toward our bus. He tapped on the bus door, and it opened right away. Mallory was only a few footsteps behind him as she followed him in.

"Hi, Mrs. Daniels and Lena. I'm Sammy."

He tilted his tall body down a little, leaned his head forward, and reached his long slender fingers forward. "Nice to finally meet you both."

Sammy, Mom, and I exchanged handshakes and a few smiles while Mallory stood back and flipped through the pages of his clipboard.

"I'm the road manager for this tour."

"So basically he knows everything. So if you need to know anything, just ask him. He is your new best friend! Sammy is going to keep us all on time just like Kay B did on the movie set, Lena," Mallory laughed. "So Lena, Sammy will catch you up on how the show will start tonight and what we have for you to do. I've gotta run and take care of a few things before I get dressed."

Mallory gave Mom and me a tight squeeze and dashed off the bus.

Sammy took a sheet from his clipboard and handed it to me. "Okay, here's the full schedule, just so you have an idea of what's happening and when."

I nodded, glanced over the sheet, and passed it on to my mom.

Sammy continued to talk. "We decided to open the show with the scene from the movie where you and Mallory first meet. It's a two-minute scene. While that's running on a big screen, you'll need to be completely ready behind the curtain."

"Okay . . ." I said cautiously. Sammy's detailed description was starting to make me feel both nervous and excited. His eyes lit up when he spoke and he looked directly at me the entire time.

"Right after the scene, the stage will go black for five seconds and the next voice we hear will be yours."

"Wow!" Mom added to the conversation.

"We want you to be full of energy and come running out, ready to have a great time! You can say something like—Hey, Texas! Are y'all excited to be here?!"

Sammy was jumping up and down and waving his hands around to show me just how he wanted it done. "Got it?" he asked.

I nodded my head vigorously, but he continued to stare at me.

"Show me!" he prompted.

Uh-oh, I thought.

"Come on, Lena, show us," Mom cheered me on. She could tell I felt weird so she winked and smiled.

"I mean—uhhhh—like—" I made a few incomprehensible sounds, raised my hands above my head, and immediately pulled them back down. "This feels weird," I said and squirmed around a bit on my feet.

I was relieved to hear Sammy laugh. "Yeah, I get it! Just be you. But we are counting on you to really get the crowd going with your energy. Okay?"

"Okay!" I raised my voice as much as I could without actually yelling. I wanted him to believe that I did know how to be energetic when necessary. Deep down inside, I was a little worried though. Suppose I really didn't have enough energy to "get the crowds going?" This wasn't going to be like filming the movie—it was live. There were no retakes or edits, just me, a big dark stage, and a room full of strangers. I needed to get this right.

Sammy was still talking, so I quickly refocused my attention to hear what was next.

"Okay, after you welcome the crowd, we want you to welcome Mallory to the stage. She will already be set up behind you. So you can just turn and do a little wide arm wave thingy, like this." Sammy raised an arm across the bottom of his belly and then slowly moved it across his body until his elbow was the only thing still touching his body.

I awkwardly mimicked him and said, "Got it."

"Okay, from there, Mallory will come out and do a few songs. When she gets to the song from the movie soundtrack, "Waters Rising," she will call you back out. This is where you share your story with everyone!"

I went numb and I'm pretty sure my heart stopped beating for at least two seconds.

"Share my story?" I questioned. I knew that is what Mallory wanted me to do, but hearing Sammy say it scared me a little. Okay, a lot.

"Yeah! You will have twenty minutes. We want you to talk about how you got the part in the movie, what you thought about the process, and a few things that God taught you or is still teaching you through all of this. Then you can finish up with a prayer. Feel free to use any scripture or specific stories that will help get your message across."

My head was nodding up and down but not purposely. *Twenty minutes?* I thought. *What would I say for twenty whole minutes?*

I glanced at Mom and silently cried, "Save me!" with my eyes.

She stepped a little closer to me and wrapped her arms around my shoulders. "Okay, so twenty minutes?" she started talking directly to Sammy.

"Yes, ma'am. Then Lena can turn it right back over to Mallory."

Mom thought for a second. "Will Mallory stay on stage with her while she shares?"

"You know, I'm sure she wouldn't mind. Would that help you feel more comfortable, Lena?" he asked.

They both looked at me. I paused and pretended to think about it even though I already knew the answer. "Yes, I think that would be good."

"Perfect. I'll talk to her," Sammy said as he wrote a few notes on the paper hanging from his clipboard. "Okay, the only other thing is after the show, you join Mallory for pictures and of course autographs. You can hang out backstage or on the bus until then, okay? All set?"

"Yes. What time do I need to be ready tonight?"

"Show's in about two hours. I'll come get you at 6:40," he said with a thumbs up. Then he darted back down the stairs and off the bus.

I collapsed onto the long brown coach and sighed. "I'm in big trouble."

Mom sat down next to me and tried to encourage me with a big smile, a tight squeeze, and soft words. "You can do all things . . ." she started.

". . . through Christ who strengthens me," I finished.

"You got it. Philippians 4:13. God has given you a story to share, so just trust that He will help you share it."

I knew Mom was right. I sat for a few more minutes breathing deeply and staring out the window. I imagined what it would feel like standing on a stage in front of hundreds of people. Or was it going to be thousands? I really had no idea, but I knew they would all be looking at me. Waiting to hear what I had to say. The scary part was that I had no idea what they wanted to hear. The entire idea seemed like a dream or maybe sort of a nightmare. The kind that doesn't makes any sense. Last week, I was riding a bumpy school bus with my best friends on the first day of middle school and today, here I am sitting on a shiny new tour bus waiting for my turn to go on stage.

I tried to picture myself running out, waving my arms, and jumping up and down like Sammy told me to do. Like I've seen Mallory and other popular singers do. I looked silly, even in my own imagination. *Maybe I'll pretend to be Emma or Ansley,* I thought to myself. *They are much funnier and a lot less shy than I am. They would be perfect up on stage.*

I closed my eyes and quietly repeated Philippians 4:13 until I felt myself start to relax a little. "I can do this," I said out loud over and over again until I forced myself to believe it. After saying it one last time, I jumped up to start getting ready. People were going to be waiting for me, and I didn't want to be late.

After thinking long and hard, I'd decided to wear my grey sweatshirt with the soft pink circles all over it. I put on a long-sleeved jean shirt underneath and left it untucked over my navy blue and white polka dot skirt. I slipped on a pair of long gray socks, scrunched them down a little and plopped each of my feet in my purple Converse.

"Ready!" I said, once I was fully dressed.

Mom stepped out from the back of the bus, "Okay, me too. You look so cute, Lena! Just let me brush your hair and we'll be all ready," she said while heading back to her room to grab the bag of hair supplies.

"Bend down," she said and began brushing my hair up into a loose ponytail. She fluffed my loose curls and patted something cold around the edges of my hairline.

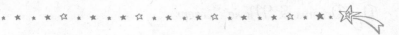

"Do you want a bow?" she asked.

"Nah," I replied. "Let's go!"

Just then, we heard a loud bang on the large bus door. "Lena, we're ready to take you in," Sammy's voice yelled from the other side of the closed door.

Mom and I dashed down the stairs and followed Sammy across the parking lot and through the back door of the church. There were wires and speakers everywhere, and people moving quickly all around us. No one seemed to even notice our entrance. They remained focused on completing whatever jobs they had been given.

"We only have about five minutes." Sammy talked quickly as he whisked us through a few tiny hallways and an open door. "Mrs. Daniels, you can sit in the audience or you may be more comfortable watching from back here in the greenroom." Sammy pointed to the large gray chairs covered with yellow and white fluffy pillows that were right in front of a large television screen. "The show will play on the screen and there are food and drinks over there. You can have whatever you'd like."

Mom smiled and thanked him.

Before Sammy could march me out of the room, Mom gave me hug and whispered, "Let's pray."

She grabbed both of my hands and said, "God, thank you for Lena. Help her to remember that everything she does is through You who give her strength. Make her comfortable and bold. Use her story to bless someone else. Amen.

"I'm watching!" she called as Sammy pulled me through another door.

Mallory was already standing there behind the large black curtain. She opened her arms wide and greeted me with a big hug. I needed that. "Breathe," she said.

Everything was moving and happening so fast. Everyone seemed to know exactly what to do and what to expect. Except me. I tried to remember everything Sammy had read off his clipboard earlier but now that it was time, it was all a blur.

"I know you want me to go on stage with you but I'm not going to. You can do it," Mallory said firmly. "You are not alone! God has given you something to say and people can't wait to hear it." She pressed one hand on my shoulder and looked directly into my eyes. "You rock, Lena Daniels!"

I started giggling and was finally feeling ready and excited. This was it. My moment to "shine." The seconds dragged. I could hear Mallory's and my voice coming from the stage, and I knew the clip from the movie had started. I clenched my fists by my sides and took a deep breath.

A few seconds later Sammy ran up behind me, handed me a microphone, and started counting, "Five, four, three, two . . . Go!"

He gave me a gentle push to jumpstart my entrance.

I peeked through the black curtains and paused. *God, help me do this,* I thought before skipping straight out to the middle of the stage. The room was quiet and dark until a big bright light was shining directly on my face and entire body.

I slowly wrung my hands back and forth around the thick black microphone. My nerves were going crazy. I paused, closed my eyes, and took a breath to try and

calm myself down. Then I slowly started to speak. "Hi, everyone!" I stuttered into the microphone. Before I could say anything else people started cheering and clapping. I heard a few shouts of my name and could even see a few people standing.

I could feel my eyes getting bigger and the nerves instantly turned into excitement and energy!

"Are you ready, Texas?" I surprised myself and shouted. "I am Lena, Lena Daniels. You may recognize me from the new movie, *Above the Waters*!" People started cheering again.

"Well, I have twenty minutes to talk to you. But just so you know, I probably won't use it all." The crowd laughed. I smiled and went on.

"I am so grateful that God gave me this opportunity. I can't believe I am in a real movie!" People started cheering again.

"So you may already know this, but I am not an actress. Well, I wasn't, but maybe I am now." I laughed at myself. "I live in Texas, and my friends and I have always loved Mallory Winston! We heard Mallory was having a contest for someone to win a chance to meet her. But really it was for a chance to audition for a part in this movie. To be honest, I really just wanted to meet her! So I begged my mom to let me enter and she said yes. I recorded a video telling Mallory a little about myself and my family and friends, but afterwards I realized I had gummy stuff in my teeth the entire time! But that wasn't the worst—I couldn't redo the video because, well, I had already sent the video in, and it was too late. And I couldn't get it back, either!"

I heard a moan run through the audience.

"But Mallory called me anyway! She said I had won the chance to audition! I sent another video in, and I actually got the part! I couldn't believe it. My entire family cried because we were all so happy, so excited. Even my dog, Austin, was super excited for me!

"Anyway, I had to miss the end of the school year, which was really hard, but thankfully my parents, my sisters, and my friends were very supportive. Filming the movie was a lot of fun, but it was really hard too. There were times when I wanted to quit, but my family and even Mallory helped me think it through. They prayed with me and encouraged me with Bible verses and stories of people in the Bible who trusted God, even when it was hard. People like Peter who walked on water. He had crazy faith and that's what I want to have! That's what God wants us all to have, because it means He can do something special and crazy with our lives."

Everyone started clapping and saying, "Amen!"

I smiled and finished up. "I learned so much about God from making this movie and really feel like I am growing in my relationship with Him. God was a friend who was there to talk to anytime I needed Him. Whenever things would get hard, I would write in my journal or pray to Him and I knew He was really there with me."

I talked for a few more minutes about the summer and then asked if I could pray with everyone before the concert started.

"Dear God, thank you for bringing these wonderful people here today. Thank you for waking me up this morning and bringing me here. I pray that no one breaks any bones—uhhh—keep us safe. Amen." I heard a few chuckles from the crowd. I couldn't believe I had actually prayed that no one would break their bones at a concert! I smiled nervously and quickly said, "Now, please welcome Mallory Winston!" And ran off the stage as fast as I could.

Mallory gave me a high five as I flew past her and headed straight for the greenroom.

Mom was standing at the door ready to greet me. "Lena! That was amazing!" she cheered. I smiled and tried not to let her see that I was actually pretty disappointed with my prayer.

"Thanks," I said, trying not to focus on how glad I was to be off the stage. I headed to the table of food and fixed a plate. I found a spot on one of the big gray chairs where I stayed for the rest of Mallory's concert. She was so fun and her voice was perfect. Each of her songs had become my favorite, and I sang along the entire time. However, every few minutes I would shake my head and think to myself, "Break any bones? Really? Who's going to break a bone tonight?"

When the show was over, Sammy came to tell me it was time to go out and meet a few fans. I cringed at the thought. I was sure no one wanted to meet me, but Sammy insisted. Mom could see the fear on my face and gave me a big hug.

"Just so you know, you didn't mess up out there," she whispered in my ear.

I was grateful for Mom's words. I nodded and we walked out together.

We reached the little booth before Mallory. There were people everywhere and they were all smiling at me. The first lady that came to meet me had tears in her eyes. She wrapped her arms around me and gave me a huge hug. It was the best hug I had had in days.

Then she looked me in the eye and said, "Thank you for sharing your story with us. I want you to know that tonight is the first time I've laughed in a very long time. I laughed because you are adorable and funny. God's love is shining on you and in you, and I needed to see it."

I thought about her smile and her words for the rest of the night. I was glad God had put me there and that I prayed for broken bones.

Before drifting off to sleep later that night, I tried to take a bite out of the very large elephant that I had tucked under my pillow. I opened to Matthew 1 and started to read: "The record of the genealogy of Jesus the Messiah, the son of David, the son of Abraham: Abraham was the father of Isaac, Isaac the father of Jacob, and Jacob the father of Judah and his brothers . . . ."

My eyes got heavy and my head drooped down until my cheek landed on the page.

Chapter 8

The sound of clicking metal woke me up. The bus was moving and it was really dark. I pushed my little curtain back and peeked out of my cubby hole bed. Outside of the nonstop clicking coming from above my head, the bus was very quiet.

I slid back into my bed and closed my eyes, wondering where we were. I had no idea how many states were between Tennessee and Missouri, but that's where we were headed next.

I hopped off my bunk and made my way to the front of the bus. Mallory and Mom were sitting at the little counter. I looked around and tried to figure out what time it was and how Mallory had managed to switch buses without me knowing it.

"Good morning, Lena," Mom turned to greet me.

"Hey, girlie," Mallory stood and gave me a pat on the back.

"So I was just telling your mom that Mr. Fenway called with a few interview requests. I told him I would check with you to see if you were up for it. We are off tomorrow, so I figured Sammy can find us a little studio where we can record them all at once."

I slid onto the little bench next to my mom.

"Ummm, okay. Sure."

"Cool. I'll see what I can find out."

"Great." I rubbed my eyes and tried to wake up a little more. Mallory and Mom both had empty cups of coffee sitting in front of them. I knew this meant they had been up for a while and were full of energy.

"I was also telling your mom that I am going to make a stop at a children's hospital on the way to our next event. I thought you might want to come too."

Mallory's face brightened as she continued to describe the events she had planned for the day at the hospital.

She said we were going to show the kids the movie and then let them ask us questions and talk about it with them. She would also sing a few songs, take pictures, color, paint nails, and just spend time doing whatever they would enjoy.

"This sounds awesome!" I told her.

We stopped a few minutes later, and Mallory headed to her own bus to get ready.

"Get ready for a fun and busy day. We will meet outside in an hour."

When Mallory left the bus, Mom and I started to get dressed. I could feel the excitement bubbling, but I also felt the little knots in my stomach that came whenever I got nervous. I started to think about the kids we were going to see.

Are they really sick? Will they be sad or too weak to smile?

I wanted to make kids smile, but, honestly, I didn't really want them to make me sad. I wasn't sure that I would be able to handle it, but I had already made my commitment to Mallory. I had to keep it.

"Mom, I'm a little nervous about this visit to the children's hospital," I said quietly.

Mom sighed lightly and nodded her understanding. "It can be difficult to put yourself in an unfamiliar situation. You have expectations, and they do too. But God's expectation is the most important. Show these kids God's love, Lena. That's what He wants. Let's pray about it."

As she prayed, Mom reminded me about the lady at the event in Nashville who had not smiled in a long time and asked that God would do the same thing with someone in the hospital.

"Dear God, we pray that you would give Lena the courage to be a light to the children that are sick. We pray that your love would fill the hearts of the doctors, nurses, parents, and kids and that Lena and Mallory would be blessed too. Amen!"

"Amen," I added and started fumbling through my suitcase. I knew I needed to wear something bright and cheery, so I pulled out a bright pink shirt and my favorite jeans. I also had a thought to grab an outfit to give to someone there. So I did, tucking the extra outfit inside of my polka dot backpack.

We saw Mallory standing outside and hopped off our bus to join her. She told us the hospital was about thirty minutes away and we would need to take a taxi.

During the drive, Mallory told me, "Lena, I am so proud of you for facing your fears last night and just being who God wants you to be. I know He is really proud of you too."

Hearing her words made me want to cry, but I held the

tears back and smiled. Mallory was very encouraging and always knew what to say to help me.

As we got out of the car, I gave her a hug and we walked in together.

As we got closer to the entrance of the children's hospital, I started to smell popcorn and something sweet. We walked in and went to the front office.

The walls were each painted a different color and lined with a combination of hand-drawn artwork, mirrors, and phrases like:

"You Are Loved."

"Welcome!"

"We can't wait to serve you!"

It was the coolest hospital I had ever seen.

"Hi! I am Mallory, and this is Lena. We are here to meet some of the kiddos," Mallory said with a cheery smile to the man at the reception area. Her eyes glistened and I could tell she was super excited. The smiling man led us to the third floor where the kids under the age of ten were staying.

When we got off the elevator, the aroma of sweets and popcorn became stronger. A lady handed us each popcorn, and I looked around.

The high ceilings had big sculptures of Minnie Mouse and a bicycle hanging from it, and balloons were flying everywhere. I could hear the metal clanking on the bike, and cheerful music greeted my ears. It was almost like an amusement park!

Children were smiling and eating cookies. Some were in wheelchairs and others were standing with braces on their legs. There were even a few kids laying on piles of blankets on the floor, but they all looked happy. It was not what I had expected at all.

All I could think to say was, "Wow!"

I guess Mallory saw the awe in my eyes. I looked at her in amazement. "It's the opposite of what you expected, right?" Mallory questioned.

"Yeah," I answered. We continued following our guide from reception. Soon we came to a big door.

"Okay, go on in," he said with a smile. "They are ready for you."

Mallory opened the door and about a dozen children were sitting, quietly waiting. When they saw Mallory's face, they starting squealing, laughing, and cheering. It was the best!

Mallory ran in waving, and I followed her as she called out, "Hey, everyone! How are you all today?"

The girls were on the pink side of the room and the boys were on the blue side. We started hugging and passing out high fives to everyone.

When the kids had all calmed down a bit, Mallory introduced herself, and told them why we were there. "Lena and I are so happy to be with you today! We are here to share some time and a very special movie with you. We hope you love it."

We found cozy spots mixed in with the kids and enjoyed our movie time.

Then for the next three hours, we laughed, giggled, and enjoyed hanging out. We even went outside and played for awhile. The kids had so much fun and my cheeks were hurting from smiling and laughing so much.

Before we knew it, our time at the hospital had come to an end. We needed to head back to the bus to get ready for that night's show.

When we announced that we had to leave, there were some tears and a lot of smiles and hugs. Instead of a sad goodbye, I went to each person and tried to say something that would make him or her laugh. As I scanned the room to make sure I hadn't missed anyone, I spotted a little girl I hadn't noticed before. She was lying on the floor in the back reading a book.

"I didn't see you outside, did I?" I asked her.

"No," she said, shyly. "I wasn't feeling great so I just stayed here and read my book."

My heart sank. I peeked at the little plastic bracelet on her arm and saw that she was my age and her name was Caroline.

"Before I leave, Caroline, I wonder if we could pray together."

Then I held her hand for a few seconds and prayed that God would help her to feel better.

When I stood up, I remembered the outfit I had thrown in my bag, and I felt as though they were meant for her. I ran over, grabbed the clothes, and brought them back over to her. I handed Caroline the colorful shirt and black leggings.

She smiled and gave me a big, soft hug. I closed my eyes and let the tears flow freely down my cheeks. I wasn't crying sad tears. I felt happy to know that God loved her so much.

"God loves you," I said. "He reminded me to bring this outfit because He wanted to see you smile!"

She giggled and pulled her new clothes close to her chest.

When I turned, I saw Mom and Mallory looking at me. Mom was shaking her head and smiling a little.

"Sorry, Mom," I said, as I got close enough for her to hear me. "I should have asked you if I could bring that outfit to share, but somehow I knew I needed to."

She hugged me and said, "Next time, just ask."

The ride back to the busses did not seem as long as the ride there had been. It might have been because I kept picturing the smiling faces we had just left. Actually I pictured those same faces for the rest of the evening. When I was on stage, I didn't think about who was in the audience, I just thought about how much God loves all of us. If He knew how happy that shirt and leggings would make Caroline, then He knew just what everyone else needed too. I prayed I would always have the courage to be who He wanted me to be—all the time.

Chapter 9

My head bobbled up and down as I sat on one of the couches staring out the window of the bus. The sun wasn't awake yet, and I had no idea what time it was. If it wasn't for the large green sign with the words "Welcome to Louisiana" on it, I wouldn't have even known where we were.

I reached over and grabbed the little piece of paper with the schedule on it and counted the cities. Being in Louisiana meant that we had already been to Missouri, Michigan, Virginia, and North Carolina.

After North Carolina, there were a few blank spaces with dates next to them and the words "Family Time" written across the empty spaces. I assumed this meant we had a break in a city somewhere, and my dad and sisters would join us! I was excited to spend a few days just hanging out with my family.

I was starting to get used to talking in front the large crowds, but meeting people after the show had quickly become my favorite part of the tour. I loved when they talked to me about what God was doing in their lives because I finally understood what Mom, Dad, and Mallory were trying to help me understand while we were filming. When my days were hard and I wanted to give up, they told me that God's plan was more than just me being in a movie. God's plans were really much bigger than anything

I could imagine. So many people were smiling and learning to trust God, and it made me smile to be a part of it.

I leaned my head forward against the window, smooshed my nose against the cold glass, and blew a kiss at the trees just for fun. The longer I sat and watched the dark empty road, the antsier I started to feel. I was excited for the day. Each city, rest stop, and church was starting to look exactly the same, but there was still something adventurous and exciting about being in each new place.

I loved watching Mallory sing. When I closed my eyes, I pictured myself on stage alongside her, singing my favorite songs. We were wearing matching purple boots and blue jeans. Halfway through the song Mallory would step back, the name on the stage would change to LENA DANIELS, and I would finish the concert on my own— dancing around the stage and singing as loudly as I could without being nervous or shy.

A long sigh escaped my lips as I pulled my head away from the glass. Dreaming about singing with Mallory made me feel all warm and gooey inside.

The bus was still silent, and the sun was still hiding. I was starting to wonder again what time it was. I used the sleeve of my sweatshirt to wipe my lip prints off the glass and tiptoed to the front of the bus.

Mr. Ernie, our bus driver, had the radio playing quietly. His eyes were focused on the road.

"Good morning," I whispered quietly.

"Hey there, sweetheart," he whispered back. "You mean goodnight?" he chuckled.

"Ummmmm . . ." I responded.

"It's only 3:30 a.m.! You need to get some sleep. Another long day is coming."

Mr. Ernie's words surprised me. I looked around at the dark roads and the quiet bus and tried to make sense of it.

"You mean it's not even close to morning yet?" I asked.

"Nope. Not yet! We've still got about eleven hours of driving left."

"Oh." I turned to walk away as Mr. Ernie offered me a little advice, "Get some rest, Lena."

"Thanks," I said and sighed quietly.

I walked toward the curtain that hid the bedrooms, using my hands to guide myself in the dark. Slowly, I crawled back into my bunk and laid with my eyes wide open. It was dark, and I could not see much of anything.

I rolled to the left and back to the right. The space between my mattress and the bottom of the bed above me was so small it was hard to get comfortable sometimes. I tossed around for a few more seconds before deciding there was no hope of getting more sleep.

No matter how hard I tried, I couldn't seem to fall back asleep. According to Mr. Ernie, I still had several hours before anyone else would be awake. My brain was racing with thoughts of our next breakfast spot, whether or not anyone would see the tiny hole in my dark blue jeans if I wore them on stage, and the fun I would have when my sisters finally arrived.

"I really wish they were here now," I whispered to myself. I knew they were having a great time with Dad and Grammy, but sleeping on a dark, moving bus still felt weird sometimes, and I didn't want to be alone anymore.

I couldn't wait to tell them about my broken bones prayer, the smiling lady in Nashville, and my visit to the children's hospital. I knew they would have stories for me too, and I was ready to hear them.

I lay still for a while longer and let my brain wander. Finally, I decided I would get a head start on next week's math assignments. Keeping up with my schoolwork wasn't as hard as I thought it would be. I normally ended up doing it while eating my lunch or while waiting for Mom to get dressed for the day. But I wasn't sure if it would be that easy when the bus was full of Ansley's giggles, Amber's stories, Ashton's singing, and Austin's barking. I figured it would be best to just get it all done. I was wide awake with not many other options.

Within 40 minutes, my math was done and I was halfway through my language arts chapter. Now I was tired enough to try this sleep thing again.

When I opened my eyes next, it was still dark in the room, and I wondered how long I had been asleep. I scooted out of bed and stepped down carefully. I slipped my feet into my fun new hot pink slippers and once again headed toward the doorway that joined my sleeping area to the front of the bus.

When I opened the curtain, I could not believe my eyes. It wasn't still dark after all. The sun was shining brightly through the large windows, and Mom was sitting at the table drinking a cup of coffee. Her Bible was sitting in front of her along with a little journal.

She looked up when she heard me shuffling through the doorway. "Good morning," she said with a smile.

"Huh?" I said. I felt really confused. "Wow. I didn't think it was morning yet!"

Mom laughed and invited me to sit with her. "Hungry?" I nodded.

I rubbed my hands across my eyes and turned to stare out the window. There was nothing there but passing cars, empty fields, and a few signs. "Wait, where's Mallory's bus?" I asked.

"In front of us. She's up and just said they'll stop whenever we are ready. I'll let Mr. Ernie know so he can tell them."

Mom slid across the little bench and moved toward the driver.

"Guess I'll go get dressed," I said loud enough for her to hear me.

As soon as I stepped back into my sleeping area, it was pitch black again and the little metal sound was still there.

I looked around the small space and remembered that we had already stored all of our luggage underneath the bus in order to make space for the rest of the family. I grunted and returned to where my mother was sitting.

Mom's face was buried in her Bible again. She looked up briefly and said, "There's a rest stop in 20 minutes, and we will get breakfast there. Okay?"

"Okay," I responded. I sat down and observed Mom as she read. Her eyebrows were wrinkled in a frown and her lips were squished together tightly. She looked like she was reading a mystery or a really good book. I wondered if she felt the same way about her Bible as Dad did. I'd tried a few times now to read my Bible, but it never got as interesting as Mom and Dad say it is. I was starting to wonder if maybe I was still doing it wrong.

I didn't want to disturb her, so I watched for a few more seconds. Her eyes moved slowly across the page. She nodded her head once as if she were having a really interesting conversation with a friend. Whenever I read my Bible it was just a bunch of big words and sentences that it seemed no one ever used in real life.

Finally, I just couldn't take it anymore. "I think something is wrong with me."

Mom looked up quickly with concern, then quickly shifted to a smile. "Because of that time you prayed that no one would break a bone?" she chuckled.

"Mom! That's not funny," I whimpered playfully. I knew from her smile that she was just teasing, so I laughed a little too. I had to admit that it did sound silly when I said it.

"Okay, okay. Seriously now. Why do you think something is wrong with you?"

"Because I can't read my Bible! I always fall asleep in the middle of the page." I felt ashamed to say it out loud. I wasn't sure whether that meant I didn't love God as much as I wanted to or should, or maybe He didn't love me as much as He loved other people. I didn't want Mom to think I was being mean, so I added, "But I love to pray!" at the end to help soften my Bible-reading confession.

"Aw, Lena. It's okay. I'm glad that you love to pray. Reading the Bible is just another way to get to know God. It's normal to not exactly enjoy or fully understand it in the beginning, but the more you read it, the more you want to know."

I was relieved that Mom didn't seem upset by my honesty, so I continued to share how I felt. "Well, I never understand what it says or what it means."

"Sometimes it's hard, but think about the Bible as a letter from God to you. So when you do like Daddy says and take a bite, you have to try to understand what God wants you to know just in that small part you read. It helps to ask questions." Mom stopped and looked at me. She was waiting for me to reply.

"Questions? Like what?"

"Let's look at the scripture we quoted last night— Philippians 4:13."

I watched carefully as Mom thumbed through the worn pages of her Bible and stopped at Philippians. She placed her pointer finger over the verse and read it out loud very slowly. She then looked at me and asked, "What do you learn about God from this one little verse?"

"Hmmmm, that I can do anything because he is strong," I responded confidently and quickly.

"Yes, but go a little deeper than just what it says. What do you know about God from this verse, even though it doesn't exactly say it?"

I didn't even try to respond with my words. I let the confused look on my face explain how I felt.

"If God gives you strength that means he is strong! And if God is strong and gives you strength then that means you are strong! But if you are strong when he gives you strength then what are you without his strength?"

"Weak?" I guessed. Mom sounded like she was speaking in a riddle, and I tried to play along.

Mom smiled. "You got it. So you are strong, Lena, only because you have someone amazing giving you that strength. Now think about how a person can give you something—if someone wanted to give you a quarter for example—but you never reached out to take it. Would you still get it?"

I shook my head.

"So, God wants to give you strength but if you want it, well, you need to get it from him! You do that by being close, spending time together—like praying, worshiping with songs, talking to others about him, and even by reading the Bible!"

Mom made reading the Bible sound so interesting. I still wasn't sure that it was going to work for me, but her excitement was contagious.

"So, according to this one little scripture, when you feel weak, then maybe it's because you are not getting the strength you need from God, even though he wants to give it to you. God has given you strength to go on stage each night, and it's because you are getting closer and closer to him. You may not feel like it, but you are."

"Wow, Mom. I don't think I can ask all those questions every time I read one verse."

Mom tilted her head down and shook it from side to side, "Like an elephant, Lena—one little bite at a time." She looked up and laughed. "Next time you read a Bible verse, just ask one question to start—ask, what does this tell me about God? The more you learn about who God is, the more the Bible starts to make sense to you."

"Okay," I said. I really wanted to be able to understand

my Bible when I read it. So even though it still may not make a lot of sense sometimes, I was willing to keep trying.

Mom looked down at her Bible for a few more seconds then shifted her eyes and hands to the little journal on her right.

"Mom?" I hesitated. It seemed like she really wanted to finish what she was doing, but I needed to ask her one more question. She kept her head down and glanced up with her eyes only.

"Did Dad talk to you about getting a devotional for me?" I said quickly.

"Yes, he mentioned it. I'm sure he will get it soon." Mom looked down and then up again. "Go grab your shoes. I'm sure we will be stopping soon. You won't have time to get into your suitcase for an outfit, but what you have on is fine." So, I jumped up quickly and did exactly what Mom said.

I missed my sisters, but there was a part of me that was happy to have some me and Mom time. Something about being alone with her reminded me that there were good parts to growing up.

Chapter 10

As soon as the bus stopped, I rushed out the bus door and inhaled the fresh air. I had no idea what time it was or how long we had been driving, but standing on the ground felt weird. My legs felt wobbly and it seemed like the ground was bouncing underneath me. I squinted my eyes a little to try to adjust to the sunlight. In front of me was a huge gas station with a large building attached to it. The red and white sign on the front said Lucy's Quick Stop. *Must be breakfast*, I thought to myself.

"Where are we?" I asked Mom as she made her way down the stairs.

"Somewhere in the Carolinas. North or South, I am not sure," she said as she led the way to Lucy's.

We were halfway across the parking lot when I suddenly felt something wet on my ankles. I was so startled I started screaming and running in circles. Mom began laughing hysterically, and I suddenly recognized Dad's hardy voice behind me shouting, "Austin, stop, boy!"

"Austin!" I screamed and tried to catch my breath. Austin's tail was wagging at a speed I had never seen before. I was still running in circles, and he was still chasing after me. He had no idea that I was running from him. When my brain finally made sense of what was happening, I convinced my legs to stand still. Austin stopped at my feet and jumped up and down on his two back legs, tapping my knees with his paws. Ansley and Ashton came running across the parking lot, and Austin and I raced towards them. Amber was a few steps behind with one shoe flopping off her foot and the other dangling in the air. We all ended up on top of each of other in one big bundle of Daniels girls with Austin yapping at each of us from the middle.

Dad flashed a huge grin and finished grabbing bags from the trunk of a long black car and tossing them underneath our bus.

As soon as he threw the last bag under our home-on-wheels, I started chanting, "Daddy, Daddy, Daddy," and created a space for him and Mom to join us.

Sammy, Mallory, and her five band members slowly started getting out of their bus and wandering around the parking lot stretching, making phone calls, and pulling bags from underneath their own home-on-wheels to get whatever they needed for the rest of the next leg of the day's journey.

Eventually we all made our way into Lucy's and began meandering around, collecting a variety of hot breakfast sandwiches, bottles of juice, cups of coffee, hot cocoa, and enough snacks to keep us energized for the rest of the day. Everyone immediately began helping Ansley, Ashton, and Amber, since Mom and Dad had stayed outside with Austin. I watched Mallory and Sammy from a distance and grabbed items similar to theirs. They always seemed to know what they were doing. I, on the other hand, did not. I didn't know when our next stop would be or what time our show was and I didn't want to end up hungry!

Once we all got what we needed, we headed back out

to the parking lot. I stayed close by the door and watched as everyone finished purchasing their breakfast or lunch. They were all wearing pajama pants, oversized sweatshirts, and bandannas. I looked down at my sky blue polka dot pajama pants and realized I fit right in. As they passed through the doors, they each greeted me with a high-five, a wink, a wave, or a pat on the head and a smile. Austin stood by my side and yelped to make sure they acknowledged him as well. It was like one big family and, somehow, I had been chosen to be part of it. In that moment I forgot all about my silly broken bones prayer, my Bible reading failures, and my wobbly legs. I knew that all of us being together would be the best part of this touring adventure.

I started thinking about how much fun Emma, Savannah, and even our new friend Joey would have had if they had come along. My new on-tour friends made me miss my old ones, and I had a sudden urge to talk to them. I had to think of a way to share the fun with them.

Mallory waltzed by everyone still in the parking lot and told us it was time to get back on the road. Mom, Dad, my sisters, and I all marched up the stairs and tried to settle in for the rest of our trip. Amber took her time, observing one area of the bus at a time while Ashton, Ansley, and Austin immediately ran from the front of the bus to the back and then to the front again, yelling out all of the cool things they saw like, "Oooh, curtains! Look at the shower! Is this my bed? That's a big refrigerator!"

Ansley stopped in the middle of the wooden floor, paused, looked around, and questioned, "Wait, where are the seatbelts? This is a moving bus, right?"

We all began laughing hysterically, including Mr. Ernie, but Dad quickly urged everyone to calm down just a bit.

"Okay, girls, we still have schoolwork to do! Don't we?" he asked.

We all moaned.

"Bye-bye, Lucy's!" Amber said as she snuggled on the long brown coach and watched as Mr. Ernie got the bus underway. I sat down next to her and wrapped my arms around her, nestling my chin on top of her head and giving her little squeeze.

Dad walked toward us and reached his arm out. He was holding a little purple bag with crinkled white and purple tissue paper overflowing from the top. "Lena, this is for you."

My eyes widened, my mouth dropped open, and out came a gasp. I had no idea what it was, but looking at the pretty purple package was all the giddiness I needed.

"Open it," Dad urged. I could tell from his smile that he was just as excited to give it to me as I was to get it.

"A devotional!" I squealed as I pulled it out of the package. The front of it was beautiful. It was cream with colorful swirls and hearts all over it. It had the words, *Spending Time with God: A Devotional for Girls* written in turquoise letters. I had no idea what was written inside, but I suddenly knew just how I could spend time with Emma, Savannah, and even Joey while I was away on this trip!

"Daddy, I love it! Can we send one to each of my friends

too? We can spend time with God together even though I'm not with them! Maybe Mom will let me FaceTime them?"

Dad's smile grew, and he answered, "Of course."

I held my new devotional close to my chest and smiled.

Dad was already on his phone ordering three more copies of the book. When he finished, he told me that later on I could write a special note for him to email to my friends. I was so excited just thinking about what I would say that I didn't want to wait.

I climbed into my bunk and grabbed my journal. The pages were almost full from my summer in California, but I managed to find a few empty pages in the back.

Just as I started to write, I could hear Ansley.

"Lena? Where are you?" she yelled.

I poked my head from behind my curtain and leaned in her direction. "Right here, but I'm busy. I'll be out later."

I watched as Ansley's shoulders sunk in and she poked her bottom lip out as far it would go.

"Leeeeennnnnnaaaaa!" she complained one last time.

I tucked my head back into my bunk and pulled the curtain forward. I listened for a few seconds as Ansley stormed back to the front of the bus and told Amber and Ashton that I didn't want to play with her.

That's not true, I thought to myself but decided not to say it out loud. I took a deep breath and refocused my thoughts onto the pages of my open journal. I wanted to write this note to my friends. Then whenever Dad was ready, I would just copy it into an email.

Hi, Guys!

I can't believe I've only been gone a week. I already miss you so much! Being on tour is super fun. The bus is not like a normal bus. Actually, I don't even think it should be called a bus. It's like a rolling house! It has everything we need on it including a TV and a really clean bathroom. I wish you could see it now, but I'll take pictures. Well, I'm sending you a surprise so watch your mailboxes! My dad got me a really cool devotional, and I think it's something fun we can all do together. I really want to read my Bible more and get to know God better, and I think this will help. Plus, it's just fun to know that even though we are doing a lot of different things, this is one thing we'll have in common! Miss you and can't wait to see you! Let's FaceTime soon!

Chapter 11

"Lena?" Mom's voice startled me. She was standing right next to my head.

"Yes, ma'am?"

"Your sisters are really excited to see you. Maybe you should spend a little time with them." Her words were soft. I paused for a moment. I knew she was right. I had just gotten so focused on telling my friends about my new devotional that I forgot how excited I was to see the girls too.

I looked at Mom. "Okay. Ansley!" I called. "Let's hang out!"

Ansley came running to the back of the bus and stood beside my bed with a huge smile plastered across her face. I pinched her cheeks playfully and climbed out of bed. "Let's make a movie," I said. Ever since I filmed *Above the Waters,* making movies with Mom's phone has been one of our favorite things to do.

"Ooo, oooo, can I be the singer?" Ansley chanted.

"I want to be in it!" Ashton and Amber joined the conversation.

I organized everyone and gave them their lines and parts to play. We arranged a few pillows on the couch to design the set, and I made sure everyone's hair was brushed. I was the director, producer, and sound technician. It was fun to sound like Mr. Fenway and say things like, "Quiet on the set, everyone!"

For what felt like hours we ran around the bus pretending to make a movie about being on tour. The bumpy roads made it a little hard for me to film my sisters without the phone camera bouncing up and down, but I pretended it didn't matter.

Just as I finished our last show, for pretend of course, Dad came to tell me it was time to get dressed for my real show.

"Can I go on stage too?" Ansley asked.

"Oh, me too!" said Ashton.

"Probably not today, girls," Dad said and continued to outline my plans for the evening. "Lena, tonight you and Mallory have a few interviews before and after the show."

"Really?" I asked. I had not had any interviews since we left California, so I wasn't expecting to do that anymore.

"Yes. There will be a few radio stations there tonight."

"So you have to be ready earlier and you will be busier than usual," Mom added.

"Okay," I said and handed Mom her phone. Ansley, Ashton, and Amber all sighed. "Sorry, guys. We can finish our movie tomorrow." I tried to cheer them up but it didn't work.

When the bus came to a stop, I grabbed my shoes and headed for the door. Mom was a few seconds behind.

"Bye, girls. Daddy will bring you in before the show starts," I yelled back to my sisters. I was excited to be on the radio with Mallory again, but I was a little sad to leave my sisters.

Sammy and Mallory met us at the back door of the church and lead us down a few hallways, telling us everything we needed to know about the night. "We'll go out to the lobby and talk to three different stations that are airing live from the show tonight. I think they gave away a few tickets, and there should be lot of girls who want to meet us."

"Airing live?" I asked. I wasn't sure what she meant.

"Oh, yeah, so you know how normally radio interviews and shows are recorded in a studio? Like we did in California this summer? Well, sometimes at big concerts and events they like to come out and talk to the artist and the crowd. They will pull different people up, give away fun T-shirts, and ask you and me some questions about the movie. It's usually a lot of fun." The excitement in Mallory's eyes made me excited too.

The closer we got to the front of the church, the more I could hear music and people laughing and talking. It sounded like a big party. We made our way through a small crowd and walked up to the back of a little booth covered with lime green and black balloons.

"And here they are! Mallory Winston and Lena Daniels!" A loud voice screamed into the microphone. Mallory jumped right into the booth, grabbed a microphone, handed me another, and started talking.

I answered a few questions, talked about how I felt being on tour, and my plans for the future. Every once in a while, I saw Sammy check his watch and whisper a few words to the man with the loud voice. Finally, he carefully whispered to Mallory, then announced that we would see everyone at the show.

He whisked us out of the booth and back down the

halls toward the back of the church. When we reached the little room where they had dinner set up, Mom and I were greeted by Dad and my sisters.

"Lena, Lena, Lena!" they squealed when they saw me. They were already sitting and eating at a small table at the back of the room. Mom headed toward them, and I waved and smiled in their direction while following Mallory and Sammy to the table with the band.

I heard Ashton mumbling, "No fair!"

Dad came over and sat next to me for a few minutes before heading back to help Mom clear the table. Sammy jumped up from where he was sitting and stood with Mom and Dad. He was explaining to them that they could stay backstage if they wanted, or they could sit in the reserved seating in the front row.

"Front row!" Amber interjected. Mom chuckled and nodded her head.

"Lena, come over and let's pray before you head out on stage tonight," Dad called to me.

Mallory stood up and asked, "Mr. Daniels, would it be okay if you prayed for all of us?"

"Certainly." Dad moved towards the center of the room.

"Can I pray too?" Ansley asked. Mallory reached for her hand and responded, "Of course! You start."

"Dear God, thank you for Mallory and for Lena. Thank you that they get to go on stage and tell people about You. Help them to do a good job and to not be shy. Amen."

Dad started as soon as Ansley finished. "God, thank you so much for each of the men and women standing in this circle. I pray that You give them the energy and talent needed to perform tonight. I pray that You would draw the audience in and that You would use these individuals to show Your love. Let them enjoy their time and keep everyone safe. In Jesus' name, amen!"

"Amen!"

Dad walked toward me, kissed me on my forehead, and told me to have fun. Ansley, Amber, and Ashton each waved and I watched as they headed to the front row to get ready for the show.

"Are you all ready?" Mallory cheered. "Lena, tonight you won't need to come back out. You can tell your testimony in the beginning, before you introduce me! Then you can hang with the family for the rest of the show. Ok?" she asked. I nodded. "Let's have a great show tonight!"

I followed Sammy to my place behind the black curtain and waited until it was time for me to head out.

As soon as I heard my name I ran out to the front and immediately scanned the front row for my family. Ansley was standing on her chair waving her hands in the air. Ashton was wrapped around Dad's shoulders and Mom was holding Amber. The crowd was loud, but I managed to hear my sisters all screaming my name.

I pointed, smiled directly at them, and said, "Hi, guys!" before I started my normal introductions. Saying hi to them first made everything easier and quicker.

I ran off stage and, instead of going to hang out backstage like I normally do, I decided to join them in the front row. When Mallory came on stage, we sang and danced just like we do at home.

Just as Mallory began singing her last song, I felt

Sammy tap me on the shoulder. "Lena," he said in my ear, "we need to get you backstage to get ready for a few more interviews."

"Ansley, let Mom and Dad know I have to go." Ansley pouted a little and tapped Dad's leg. Sammy gave him a thumbs up and whisked me away.

By the time Mallory finished, Sammy and I were waiting. He led us down the halls, and Mallory and I picked up where we'd left off before the show started—smiling, taking pictures, and answering questions from a lot of people.

The day was long and I was tired, but being in the middle of so much fun gave me all the energy I needed to make it through the rest of the night.

Chapter 12

"Great job tonight, Lena," Mallory yelled from across the parking lot as we all headed toward the busses.

I turned and flashed a huge grin. "Thanks, you too!"

"See ya in a few days! We're headed to the country next. Hope you brought your cowboy boots!" Sammy joined in the conversation. I wasn't sure what he was talking about because I didn't own any cowboy boots. I waved at them both, opened the large door, and dashed up the stairs, chuckling at Sammy's words.

"What's so funny, Lena?" Ansley was sitting at the table waiting for me.

"Nothing," I answered, walking past her. I could hear her little feet pitter-pattering behind me.

"Lena, tell me!" she demanded.

"I said nothing! I was talking to Mallory," I snipped.

"That's all you ever do now," she complained. "You never talk to me!" she screamed and stormed to the front of the bus. Dad came through the doorway from the back of the bus with Ashton and Amber close behind. Mom stayed back, but I knew she was listening.

"What's going on out here?" he asked.

Amber and Ashton were wearing pink and purple pajamas covered in little hearts and circles with matching polka dot scarves on their heads. Dad turned quickly and told them to go back with Mom and finish getting ready for bed.

"Lena is being mean to me!" Ansley shouted to Dad with a face full of instant tears. She pouted and waited for Dad to step in and rescue her.

"No, I'm not," I replied before Dad had a chance to say anything. I refused to lose just because she was in tears. I let out a long deep moan and accidentally let a few tears fall down my own cheeks. "That's not true! I just got back, and I'm really tired."

Dad looked at both of us and said, "Girls, this is our first night together on the bus. Is this really how you want to spend it?" I crossed my arms and focused my attention on the little lights that lined the edge of the ceiling.

"Does Lena get to stay on tour when we leave?"

Dad nodded.

"She gets to do everything!" More tears streamed down Ansley's face and looking at the ceiling could no longer help me pretend not to notice.

I could feel my heart breaking into tiny little pieces as I watched Ansley's meltdown. No matter how upset I was, I could never handle seeing my sisters cry.

I searched for the right words to erase her tears, but all I came up with was, "That's not true, Ansley." I softened my tone and hoped it would make her feel better.

I dropped my head when I heard her moan get even louder than it had been the first time.

Dad stood quietly for a few more seconds before squatting down to get closer to our height.

"Ansley," he said gently. "I know you've missed your sister, but let's see if we can focus on the good things. Like you get to be with her now!"

"There's nothing good for me!" Ansley snapped quickly.

"Ansley, stop it. That's not true." I stooped down a little and tried to look her in the eyes. She looked away and refused to look back. "Well, fine then!" I yelled and turned to walk away.

Dad called me back and told us to both go sit on the couch. Then he called for Mom, Ashton, and Amber to come join us.

"Family meeting time," he said. Ansley sat on one end of the couch, and I sat on the other. We made sure we were as far apart as possible. Austin plopped himself underneath my feet.

When Ashton and Amber ran out to join us, Ashton reached down and scooped Austin up under his belly. Then they sat between us. Austin ran from one end of the couch to the other smacking our faces with his tongue.

"Ashton, why did you pick him up? Just put him down!" I said as I scooped him in my arms and placed him back on the floor.

"You're so mean!" Ashton screamed and scooted closer to Ansley.

Mom and Dad sat on the shorter couch across the wide wooden floor. Then Dad looked at each of us before he began speaking. "Guys, I know things have been a little crazy this week."

"Yup!" Amber said. She was the only one with a smile still plastered across her face.

"We've been apart, and we haven't really had a lot of time together. Does anyone miss our regular life?" We all sort of said yes with various grunts and moans. Dad did not push for a clearer response but continued talking.

"Yeah, but here's the thing, guys—God has us all back together now. And even though we haven't had our normal lives, there are things we can be grateful for and choose to be happy about anyway. But it's a choice."

"But Lena is always happy when she's not with us." Ansley had decided she wasn't ready to move on just yet.

"Ansley, I know it's hard being a little sister sometimes. Mommy was a little sister too. But there are also a lot of fun things about being younger! Like having someone to look up to and learn from. Just like Dad said, you get to choose what you focus on—the parts that make you happy or the stuff that you don't like."

Dad spoke up as soon as Mom finished. "Instead of being sad that we only have a few days on the bus together, let's find a way to celebrate and create really fun memories. Maybe tonight we can create a list of things we can do over the next few days. Tomorrow Lena does not have a show, so we can start checking things off our list!"

"Let's paint our nails," Ashton shouted.

"Or play hide and seek," Amber chimed in.

Soon enough, Ansley spoke up too. "Can we watch a movie tonight?" Mom paused and gave Dad a soft smile. Dad couldn't hold back a grin. He looked at Ansley, winked, and said, "Okay. Movie night it is!"

We decided to ask Mr. Ernie if we could make an extra stop to buy something fun to do. Of course he agreed.

I ran to put on my purple one-piece pajama set with the yellow smiley face covering the long zipper down the front. Ansley decided to wear hers too. When we felt the bus slowly turning, and eventually stopping altogether, we rushed to the door and raced into a huge store with Mom and Dad following close behind us. We headed straight for the freezers and grabbed the largest tub of ice cream we could find. We passed an aisle with games and toys, and Amber spotted a safari-themed jumbo puzzle that she insisted we needed.

"So, are we going to make it a game night instead?" Dad asked.

"That puzzle won't take that long," I said, shaking my head. "Can we get a movie too?"

"Let's get two!" Mom added.

We all strolled to the middle of the store toward the giant bins of DVDs. Our feet shuffling along the tan tiles reminded me of Austin's little paws dragging across our hardwood floors at home. "Guys, let's get Austin a . . ."

"Lena, look!" Ashton cut me off mid-sentence, as she squealed and started jumping up and down. All of our eyes immediately followed her pointing fingers to the ceiling.

"Whoa!" Dad exclaimed. Mom's mouth dropped open, and I blinked a few times really fast to make sure I wasn't imagining what I saw. But there it was. My face was on a large plastic poster hanging above our heads.

The words "Now in theaters: *Above the Waters*" were in huge black letters underneath a picture of Mallory and me.

I froze a moment, and then immediately looked to make sure Ansley was okay. I let out a sigh of relief when I saw that her smile was bigger than mine.

"I like Mallory's hair," Amber noted. "And you look pretty, Lena."

"Thanks, but this feels so weird! Let's get our movie

and go." We all laughed and quickly agreed to get the movie with a girl, a horse, and a dog on the cover.

We made it all the way through checkout, out of the store, and were just about to open the door of the bus when I heard a little girl whisper and start pointing in my direction.

"Excuse me! Are you Lena Daniels?"

"Uhhhh." I gulped and tried to move a little quicker. Ashton opened the door of the bus and climbed the stairs.

"Hi!" Dad wrapped his arm around me to stop me from getting on the bus and spoke first. His voice was chipper, and he sounded so kind. "Yes, this is Lena Daniels. Have you seen the movie? Hope it was a blessing to you!"

The little girl started giggling, and the tall lady holding her hand answered Dad, "Yes! Oh, my goodness, we just saw it the other night. There was an advanced screening for some of the families at our church and the whole family was able to attend! God really touched my heart after seeing it. She did such a good job."

I smiled and waved at the giggling little girl with two bouncing ponytails.

"I like your shoes," she said while pointing at the little monster faces hanging off my fuzzy blue slippers.

I looked down in shock. I completely forgot that I was in my pajamas!

"Do you mind if we take a picture with Lena?" the lady asked my dad.

"Oh, yeah, no problem," Dad answered for me. Somehow he managed to completely miss how mortified I was. I looked at him and hoped he would notice the embarrassment in my eyes. I was wearing a fuzzy one-piece pajama set and no one seemed to care!

The giggly girl and her mom stood close. I took a few steps back and tried to hide my entire body behind the little girl, but Mom motioned for me to step forward.

"Lena, we can't see your face!" she said.

Mom and Ashton moved over just enough to make sure I was the only one being photographed in purple pajamas.

"Say cheese!" the lady said out loud while Dad held the little phone in the air and pointed it directly at us.

I forced my teeth together and tried to pretend I didn't feel ridiculous. But before Dad could snap the picture, I saw a four-legged bundle of fur bolting down the steps of the bus just behind him.

"Austin!" I yelled and jumped forward to try to catch him. He zoomed right past my flailing arms, spun in three quick circles around the lady's feet, and yelped over and over again. The little girl started screaming and climbed up her mother's legs.

Mom reached out and tried to grab him. Ashton copied her failed attempts, but Austin escaped both of them and took off, zig-zagging across the parking lot.

"Austin! Come! Come now!" Dad shouted. Austin completely ignored the commotion he had caused and continued on his journey.

"Austin, stop!" I demanded without success. He went straight through the open doors of the big store, down the middle aisle, turned to the right, and came back up the next aisle. One-by-one, we frantically followed after him in our pajamas. The little monsters on my slippers and the little pigs on Ansley's moved super fast as we tried to catch our dog. The faster we ran, the faster he ran. A few people in the store joined our escapade and placed themselves at the tops and bottoms of the aisles until we finally heard a man yell, "Got him!"

Austin hung from the man's arms with his tongue dangling out of his mouth and his short tail whisking frantically from side-to-side. Everyone started cheering and laughing. I grabbed Austin and thanked the helpful stranger. He smiled and said, "Cool slippers!"

I tried to hide my embarrassment and said, "Oh, thanks."

"Thanks, everyone." Dad waved at the crowd and flashed a huge grin before leading us back out of the store, across the parking lot, and onto our bus. I waited for everyone else to get on and was sure to pull the door closed behind me.

"Well, that's one fast pup you have there!" Mr. Ernie said from his seat at the wheel. "I didn't even know he ran off until I saw everyone running across the parking lot! What a sight!" He let out a deep belly laugh and buckled his seat belt.

Dad stood at the front, talking and laughing with Mr. Ernie while we settled in for our night of family fun.

Chapter 13

Mr. Ernie dropped us off at a hotel in Nashville for the weekend. Our one movie night turned into two, and then kept going for each night at the hotel.

Mr. Fenway scheduled a few radio interviews for Mallory and me that we needed to do during our few days off. They didn't take very long, and sometimes they were done over the phone. Mallory offered to do them without me so that I could spend more time with my family, but I told her I didn't mind. Mom and Dad didn't mind either, and it actually turned out to be a lot of fun.

Everyone seemed to ask us the same questions, but I didn't mind repeating my answers over and over again. Talking about *Above the Waters* and my summer in California helped me remember how excited I was when I first met Mallory. And Dad said sharing my testimony was a great way to remind myself of how God had answered my prayers.

My last interview was in a really tall building that looked like it was covered in mirrors. The entire family was with me. Well, everyone except for Austin. We left him in his crate at the hotel. He was pretty tired from the excitement on the bus and needed the rest anyway.

Mallory texted Mom and told her she would meet us at the elevator doors, and that's exactly where we found her.

"Hey, guys!" she was always so chipper when she

greeted us. Everyone exchanged hugs, then we loaded into the mirrored elevator and made our way to the radio station on the fourteenth floor.

"So—" Mallory started to speak. "Ansley, I was thinking maybe you would want to join in our interview today. People always ask about Lena's family, so why not let them meet one of you!"

Ansley's eyes basically popped out of their sockets and her mouth opened wide. "What?" she asked anxiously.

"Would you like talk on the radio today too?" Mallory repeated it.

"Oh, no. I can't!" she yelped.

"Huh? Yes, you can!" I urged her.

"No. I don't want to do it. I'm too scared."

"Awww, okay," Mallory said, sounding a little disappointed.

Mom and Dad gasped. "Ansley, it will be so fun! You don't have to be scared," Dad added.

Ansley shook her head and ignored us as we all pleaded with her.

"Okay then. Just let me know if you change your mind," Mallory said as she led the way off the elevator and to the studio where we would record the show.

When everyone else went in, I tapped Ansley on the shoulder and stood close to her. "Ansley, you know you don't have to be scared, right?" I said. "I was scared the first time I had to do this too, but I am so glad I did it anyway. I think you should ask God to help you not be afraid. That's what I do."

I watched as Ansley's face began to relax a little. "And

I'll be right there with you," I assured her. Once I said that, Ansley smiled and nodded her head. "So, is that a yes?" I asked.

She nodded again. "Yay!" I cheered. "Want to pray first?"

Ansley reached out her hands and closed her eyes. "Dear God, thank you for Ansley! She is so brave and beautiful and I know you have great plans for her. Will you give her the courage to do things even when they seem scary just like you did for me?" I squeezed Ansley's hands and added, "Oh, and God, will you help her to have fun too? In Jesus' name, amen!"

When we opened our eyes, Ansley was bursting with excitement. We pushed through the doors and met up with Mallory, who didn't seem surprised to see Ansley with me. She introduced us to Kelly, the radio show host who would be talking with us, and headed for our interview.

After answering questions about where and when the movie was filmed, she introduced Ansley and brought her into the conversation. I watched as Ansley laughed and chimed in with funny stories. I was so glad that she didn't let being afraid stop her from having such a good time.

When we finished, Mallory let Ansley know how proud of her she was. Ansley could not stop smiling!

To celebrate the fun interview, Dad treated us all to ice cream at a really big park near our hotel. We made sure to bring Austin along for all the fun. But for this outing we kept him on his leash to make sure he didn't escape again!

That was just the beginning of a much-needed break from stages and microphones.

We spent the next four days exploring the city of Nashville. Mom and Dad took us to the aquarium, the movies, and the science museum. We ate a lot more ice cream and spent a few afternoons playing on the swings and sliding down the slides at the park.

One evening, I asked if I could FaceTime my friends. I wanted to know if they had received their devotionals, and I also just wanted to see their faces. Mom and Dad agreed.

The hotel room was pretty small, so Mom thought it was best to walk me down to the lobby. Thankfully, it wasn't too noisy there. I was so excited to talk to them. Mom tried Emma's mom first, but we didn't get an answer. Next we tried Savannah. I couldn't believe my eyes when she answered. She was with Emma and Joey! They were all smiling and giggling before I even said a word.

"Lena!" Emma screamed. "We miss you!"

"I miss you too, guys! But no fair! Are you having a sleepover?" I pretended to cry but they just laughed at me. I couldn't pretend to be sad for long and ended up laughing with them.

"Wait, isn't it a school night?" I asked in a more serious tone.

I watched as the smiles started to fade. Emma nodded and looked away.

"Yeah, Joey's dad had to work and asked my mom if she could come over . . . so we made it a sleepover."

"Wow, that's really nice! I can't believe everyone's mom actually agreed to that!" I shouted.

"Well," Joey sat up a little. "My mom is actually in Florida. She went back for a few weeks."

I gasped. I wasn't sure what I needed to say next. Thankfully Savannah spoke up.

"Lena, Joey may be moving back to Florida. Things aren't working out with her Dad's job."

I blinked really fast a few times.

"It's okay though," Joey tried to smile. "We don't know yet. Mom just went back to see my grandmom and check on our house. We never sold it, and now we may be able to move back into it." She paused, "I mean if we move back. I don't really know what my Dad will decide. He may be able to get his old job back. I'd go back to my old school and everything would be just like it was before we moved."

I just sat and listened to Joey. She was trying to sound positive, but as she talked her eyes started to water a little. I had to admit this was not the news I was expecting to hear when I called them tonight. I was really liking the idea of having a new girl for our friend group.

"I'd really miss you guys though. I've never had friends like you before."

Emma wrapped her arms around Joey's shoulder. "Hey there," she said. "You can't get rid of us that easily! We'd figure out a way to visit and FaceTime, just like we are now! Don't worry about it!" She squeezed Joey until she smiled again.

So, Lena, how's the tour? Tell us everything!" Savannah shouted in a voice louder than her normal one. I knew she was just trying to cheer us all up by changing the subject, but it felt weird to talk about that now.

"Well, you will have to wait for me to get home to tell you *everything*, but I'm having a lot of fun," I answered.

"Tell us something else then!" Joey demanded with a huge smile.

"Well, Mallory is even cooler on tour than she was on the movie set. And the band and tour manager are really fun too."

They all leaned in really close to the screen and waited for me to say more.

I told them about my nervousness on stage the first night, the interviews, and the fun crowds of people. "Lena!" Emma shouted. "That's sounds so fun!" I had to agree. Hearing myself talk about all the things I'd been able to do felt weird, but it definitely sounded fun! We talked for just a little while longer. They listened and we all laughed until I heard Savannah's mom in the background telling them that it was time to say goodnight.

"Mom says we have to go. Lena, can you call us tomorrow too?" Savannah said.

"I can try!"

"Oh, Lena!" Emma jumped in. "We got our devotionals, and we love them! Thank you so much for sending them!"

"Oh, yeah!" Savannah added. "It's been really good! I can't remember what day I am on, but the one about caring for others is my favorite, and the one about how friends are a gift!"

"Mine too! It reminds me of us!" I shouted.

"Yeah, let's keep reading it even after you get back," said Savannah. "Joey has been reading hers too."

"Good idea!" I agreed. We exchanged a few more smiles and finally said, "See ya later!" before hanging up.

My friends felt like family, and I loved getting to see their faces even though we were so far apart.

My family finished our time together with one last night on the bus so that it would be easier for Mr. Ernie to drop my Dad and sisters off at the airport. Then Mom and I would continue with the rest of the tour. Even though our time together had been short, we had a lot of fun. Everyone was sad when it was time for them to head home, but they knew Grammy was waiting for them.

Mom and I stood on the sidewalk outside the airport and waved goodbye. I squeezed my eyes shut tight and tried not to cry as I watched my Dad, Austin, and my sisters head through the glass doors.

"Not much longer and you will be with Grammy and everyone too," Mom whispered to me.

She was right. There was only one week before I would be with them again. What she didn't realize was that my tears were mixed with feelings of missing them and fears of missing the tour once it was over. I was actually enjoying this new way of life, and now it was almost done. I loved going to bed not knowing where I would wake up.

Mom wrapped her smooth, brown fingers around mine, and we turned to go back to the bus. The door was open wide, and I could see Mr. Ernie wasn't sitting in his seat behind the wheel like usual.

I ran up the wide stairs and was immediately welcomed by the smell of lemons and daisies. Mr. Ernie was wiping a rag across the leather sofas.

"Hey, there," he looked a little startled by our arrival. "Just giving the ol' boy his weekly cleaning."

Mom laughed, "Yeah, I know what you mean! Can't

imagine what our real house will look like after me being gone these last weeks!"

Mom and Mr. Ernie laughed so hard, and I felt a little ashamed and responsible for the mess we'd made.

"Sorry for our mess," I said while walking toward him. "Now that my sisters are gone it won't be as messy." I reached my hand out for his can of lemony spray.

"Oh, no sweetie! I don't mind you or your sisters at all. I've had more fun watching and listening to you girls and that dog than I have had in a long time! You guys are special. I'll miss them and you too, young lady."

Mr. Ernie's face was bright, and I could see all his teeth as he grinned. I wondered what his life was like when he wasn't driving this bus. Mom must have been thinking the same thing. "Aww. We will miss you too. Do you have kids, Mr. Ernie?" she asked.

"Oh, yes, I sure do." He reached into his back pocket and pulled out a little cracked black wallet and opened to a tiny picture. "These are my boys. They are all grown up now." He flicked his wallet in the air until the plastic flaps holding the picture flipped over. "And these are my grandchildren."

"Oh, they are all beautiful!" Mom leaned in.

"Yeah," Mr. Ernie said proudly. "But you see, I don't live near my boys. So, I don't get to see them or my grandkids that often. That's why I've loved having y'all on the bus so much. Reminds me of them."

"Awww!" I smiled and kept listening. Mr. Ernie wasn't finished yet.

"Yeah, I drive a lot of people around. Lots of musicians.

But not a lot of them are like y'all, and they make a way dirtier bus than this."

I watched curiously as Mr. Ernie gently took the can from my hand and moved from the couches to the countertop next to the big black refrigerator. Mom was shaking her head like she knew exactly what he was saying. I wasn't sure, so I decided to ask.

"Mr. Ernie, what do you mean 'not like us?'" I stepped a little closer to him.

He looked at Mom and let out a nervous laugh before he answered. "Well, they aren't always nice to me or to anyone else. And they like to party but in a bad way. They make huge messes with food, cans, and all kinds of trash. Nothing like you girls and your little cookie crumbs! I don't mind helping you and sweeping those up one bit!" He flashed me quick grin.

"Mr. Ernie, can I ask you a question?" I said.

"You sure can," he answered.

"Do you know God?" The words came out of my mouth before I had a chance to think about it. I wasn't sure what made me ask him that, but once I did I was completely nervous and embarrassed. I didn't want to upset him or make him uncomfortable. I tried to erase the words with a follow up, "Ummm, I mean . . ." but it was too late. Mr. Ernie was already preparing his answer.

"You know, it's funny that you ask me that. It's been a long time since I've been in church or anything. I used to know Him, but I've done a lot of not-so-good things since then." Mr. Ernie hung his head low and shook it from side to side. "But I've been coming in and watching you, young lady, when you go into these big churches all across the country and talk to thousands of people about Him. And I wonder what I'm missing."

"You've been watching me?" My eyes lit up and I suddenly felt a little giddy. I had no idea Mr. Ernie ever even left his bus.

"Oh, yeah. You think I could just stay on this bus while my new favorite family was doing something special? Oh, no. I stand in the way back every night by the door and listen. I like Mallory too. I bought a few of those CDs and sent them to my granddaughters. I want them to meet you one day and be like y'all as they grow up."

Wow, I thought. Every word Mr. Ernie was saying hit me in a special place in my heart and sent little tingling feelings down my arms.

I looked at Mom. Her face was glowing and her eyes were filling with tears.

Mr. Ernie kept talking. "I guess I do need to talk to God more and get to know Him a little better."

I wasn't really sure what to say next. I wished Mallory was here. She would know just what to say. I felt my nerves coming back. Mr. Ernie turned and continued to spray and wipe the counters, but I couldn't stop thinking that there was something more I needed to say or do. I looked at Mom for help, but her eyes were closed and her cheeks were wet.

God help me, I thought to myself.

"My dad says that getting to know God is like eating an elephant," I said, blurting out the one thing I knew was right because it's what Dad had told me.

Mr. Ernie stopped wiping and looked at me. "Well,

you're going to have to explain that one to me, young lady."
He chuckled.

I sighed and smiled, "You just take it one bite at a time! And I think the more you eat, the yummier God makes it for you!"

"Ahhh, is that right?" Mr. Ernie's smile was big, and he kept chuckling.

"Yup! And you don't even have to feel bad about the not-so-good things you've done. I do that all the time. But in the Bible, God tells us that He forgives us when we ask Him to and that He's the only one that can help us to not do those things anymore."

I wished I knew where that was in the Bible, but I couldn't really remember.

"Mom, what scripture is that again?"

She slowly looked over at me and smiled softly. "Well, Psalm 103:12 says he has removed our sins as far from us as the East is from the West. And Romans 8 tells us that the Spirit helps us in our weakness when we don't even know what to ask for. There are many others, so Mr. Ernie, Lena is right. God's always ready to forgive us and help us."

"Can we pray for you, Mr. Ernie?" I blurted out again without thinking.

Mr. Ernie immediately put his rag down and stood tall. "Young lady, I'd sure love that. Mr. Ernie is an old man, but what a great example you are to me. You are special, and I think it's because of God. I'd like to have that too."

Without any hesitation, I reach forward and grabbed one of Mr. Ernie's hands. Mom stepped closer and grabbed the other one.

I closed my eyes tight and forced all of my nerves to the bottom of my stomach until I could no longer feel their presence.

"Dear God, thank you for Mr. Ernie. I am sorry for not cleaning up our mess better, but I am grateful that Mr. Ernie shares his bus with us and that he is so nice. Will you help Mr. Ernie to know how much you love him? Will you help him to know that when he asks you, you will forgive his sins and make him feel happy? Thank you, God, for always loving us no matter what. Will you keep Mr. Ernie and his sons and grandchildren safe? And I pray that they will all know you and love you. In Jesus's name, amen."

Before I finished praying, I could hear Mr. Ernie sniffling. He let go of my hand and reached into his back pocket to pull out an old white handkerchief. He wiped it across his eyes before looking up.

"Thank you," he said. "Thank you. Thank you." He said it the exact same way as he had before.

I moved a little closer and wrapped my arms around Mr. Ernie's waist. I was so glad to be on his bus. It really felt like he had become part of our family now.

Mr. Ernie wrapped one arm around my shoulder and squished me under his arm. "Well, guess somebody needs to drive this bus! You've got people waiting to see you in Atlanta tonight!"

Mom patted Mr. Ernie on his shoulder as he walked by. I could see the leftover tears on her cheeks. They had formed little streams from the corners of her eyes down to the bottom of her jaw.

Mom opened her arms wide. She pulled me in close,

and I sunk my head into the middle of her chest for a quick moment as our house-on-wheels turned out of the Nashville airport parking lot.

"Lena, I'm so amazed by how God is using you," Mom said as she held my face between both of her hands. "It's about so much more than that movie, Lena. So much more."

She kissed my wet cheek and told me she was going to go lay down.

I wasn't sure how long of a drive we had to Atlanta, but I knew it was daytime, and I wasn't sleepy.

I went to my bunk and grabbed my black journal, my Bible, and the new devotional Dad had gotten me. Then I found a cozy spot on the freshly cleaned brown leather couch. I pressed my face to the window just in time to see the green sign that read, "Atlanta 245 Mi."

"It'll be a while," I said to myself, as I opened the journal across my lap and started to write a note to my friends.

Hey, Girls!

I really miss you but we only have a few more days. Tell me what I'm missing in school! Have you been reading your devotional? Don't feel bad if you've missed a day or two, I know it's hard, but just do it whenever you can. I think God really wants us to do it together. Today the weirdest thing happened. I prayed for our bus driver! We have been riding with him all this time, and we didn't know anything about him. At first, I felt really bad because he was cleaning up after Dad, Ashton, Amber, and Ansley left. But then Mom and I started talking to him.

*We saw pictures of his family and started talking
to him about God. At the end, we prayed for him,
and I'm going to keep praying for him every day! It
reminded me of the first devotional in the book that
tells us how important it is to take time and care for
others. I am so glad I took time to care about Mr.
Ernie, because hopefully now he will know God!
Can't wait to hear who you've been caring for!*

I stopped writing long enough to flip to the first page of
the devotional. I really wanted to know scripture and have
them memorized like Mom and Dad, but I didn't yet. So
I copied the verse from the little box at the bottom of the
page into my journal too.

Philippians 2:4

*"Let each of you look not only to his own interests,
but also to the interests of others."*

Chapter 14

From our window, I watched as Mallory's bus turned into the parking lot and pulled up right next to ours outside of a big, red brick building.

It turns out 245 miles is really only about four hours, so we arrived in Atlanta before I even had a chance to take a little nap!

When I felt the bus stop, I jumped up, bent my back forward a little, and stretched my arms out long in front of myself.

I continued to stare out the large window as Mallory and the band bounced down the stairs smiling and laughing. They all looked like they were having so much fun.

A few went directly to the side of the bus and opened the large metal doors revealing luggage, speakers, and lot of other equipment. Others just stood around smiling and talking.

I tried to stop watching but I couldn't. I was really hoping that Mallory, Sammy, or any of them would notice me gawking and invite me to join them. No one did. They continued to move about with purpose and never even glanced in my direction.

I was so focused that I didn't even notice Mom coming up behind me.

"Lena," she said. Her words startled me, and I squealed.

"Oh, my!" Mom laughed. "Well, why don't you go say hi? You haven't seen them in a few days."

I heard Mom, and I really wanted to, but I had a gazillion thoughts scattering through my brain. *What if they didn't want me to? What if they just ignored me? What if they just kept talking to each other when I got there? What if I couldn't think of anything to say?*

Mom must have seen my brain working really hard because she interrupted my thoughts and said, "Just go do it. I know you don't want to be stuck on this bus with me anymore!"

She was right. Not about me not wanting to be stuck on the bus with her, but about me really wanting to go talk to the rest of the tour group. We had already finished two weeks of the tour and, outside of quick hellos and hugs, I had not talked to Mallory much at all. I'd been spending a lot of time with my family, and I knew she was always really busy getting ready for each night and its performance. Today felt different, and as I watched her interact with everyone else, she looked more relaxed than usual. Maybe it was because we normally arrive in a new city with just enough time to get dressed and run on stage, and today it felt like we still had hours before the evening's event.

"What time is it, Mom?" I asked.

Mom looked surprised by my question but she answered anyway, "It's only noon and . . ."

"Oh, wow!" I cheered. We had more time than I thought.

Mom finished her thought, "I know. Dad and the girls are already back home and the girls even made it to school this morning!"

"Whoa," I said calmly. Of course, I was listening to

Mom, but mostly I was building up enough courage to step off the bus. "I'll be back!" I said and raced down the stairs before my brain could stop my feet from moving.

As soon as I turned into the space between the two busses, I could hear Mallory shouting my name. "Lena! Hey!" she called playfully, skipping toward me and giving me a big squeeze.

I could hear Sammy and the others calling my name and welcoming me back on tour too. I let out a deep sigh and smiled big. I noticed Mom standing in the big window, so I gave her a little wink and wave to let her know I was going to be okay.

"How were your days off? I know it was just a little while, but did you have good time?" Mallory asked.

"Yes! We hung out in Nashville and saw some pretty cool places."

"Oh, fun! Wish I could have stayed and hung out with you. Feels like I haven't even seen you or had the chance to just talk for a bit." She made a silly face when she finished.

"Yeah, it's okay. How was your break?" I responded naturally. Talking to her reminded me that we had actually become friends, and I didn't need to feel nervous around her.

"Oh, it was busy." She laughed. "But good. I'm working on my next CD, you know, so it's a crazy time for me."

"Wow." I had forgotten that Mallory was recording her concerts to use as part of her new CD. No wonder she seemed so distracted and was so focused while performing.

"Guys, let's go!" Sammy yelled to Mallory.

Mallory looked up at the bus and asked if my sisters were still with me. When I told her no, she asked if I wanted to have lunch and hang out with everyone for a little while before the show. She invited Mom too.

I ran up to the bus and asked Mom if she wanted to join us, but she declined. She was sitting across the table from Mr. Ernie with her Bible open.

"Enjoy yourself, sweetie," she said.

A silver van pulled up, and Mallory and the others headed toward it. I hurried and joined them. I climbed in, went all the way to the back, and plopped between Mallory and her drummer. The others filled in the open seats in the middle, and Sammy hopped in the front with the driver.

He looked at the driver and said, "Hey, man! So, where can we get some good sushi?"

Sushi? I thought. *Ew.*

It was as if Mallory could read my mind. While Sammy and the driver continued to talk, she turned in my direction and patted my knee. "I'm sure they will also have fried rice with chicken or something you'll like."

I sat quietly and smiled. I hoped she was right. I had not eaten anything since our 9:00 a.m. rest stop. My stomach was starting to let me know how it felt about that, and I wasn't sure how it would feel about a plate of raw fish.

When we arrived at the restaurant, I spotted a burger joint and a taco bar, and experienced a momentary sense of relief, followed quickly by the realization that in between them was a place with a tiny red sign that said, "Zen."

"There it is," Mallory announced with excitement when she spotted it. I sighed and followed the group out of the van and into the tiny restaurant. I slid into a booth next to Mallory and quickly ordered my fried rice and chicken.

I sat quietly for most of the meal, pondering the level of skill needed to pick up slimy pieces of red, white, and orange fish with chopsticks.

"Want some?" Sammy asked. I passed.

"Oh, just try it!" Mallory encouraged me.

I gave in and took a piece of raw pink fish wrapped in rice from Mallory's plate. I closed my eyes, put it in my mouth, and chewed. When I opened my eyes, everyone was staring at me. I pretended to gag and everyone groaned. Then I smiled.

"It's good!"

"Yay!" everyone cheered.

"Just a little slimy."

Mallory ordered me a sushi roll of my own, but with shrimp. That way I didn't have to eat another slimy one.

In the middle of our meal Mallory's phone rang. It was Mom.

Mallory hurried away from the table to talk. When she came back I could tell that something wasn't right. She said I had a family emergency, and I needed to get back to the bus.

When I got back, my mom was in tears. Everyone was silent. I was the only one smiling since I had no idea what was going on. I looked around and wondered what they all knew that I didn't. Mom told me to sit down.

I looked at Mom and she quickly glanced at me and then glued her eyes to the ceiling. She was trying to stop tears from welling up in order to talk to me.

Not able to take the suspense any longer, I asked, "What happened?"

She didn't move her eyes. She didn't shift her body. "Mom . . ." I said.

"It's Grammy. Dad had to take her to the hospital." She looked at me and more tears began to roll down her cheeks.

I sat there staring at her, not knowing whether to say something, grab her, or to just sit still. I knew Grammy got sick sometimes, and this certainly wasn't her first time in the hospital. But the look on Mom's face made me afraid.

Mom saw the worry in my eyes and said, "The doctors say she's going to be okay, but I still think it's best for us to go home. I'm sorry."

Tears started to stream down my face. Mom took me in her arms and hugged me tightly. It could probably have set a world record for the longest hug. But it felt good. Mom's arms around me gave me a peace that I can't explain, and the way she held on tight made me think I did the same for her.

Sammy and Mallory met us back on the bus and gave Mom our new flight information. They had taken care of everything for us. I tried to tell Mallory I was sorry that I would not be able to finish the tour with her, but she told me to shush and gave me a long hug.

"Family is everything," she said.

"Let's pray for you guys before you go," Sammy said and led us off the bus so that everyone could join in. We stood in a large circle and held hands. Mr. Ernie stood next to me and wrapped his arm around my shoulder.

Mallory prayed, "Lord, we thank you for Mrs. Daniels and Lena and their entire family. Right now we ask that you comfort them as they travel back home. We ask that

you would give them smooth and safe travels. I also pray
that you would heal Grammy. We are so grateful to know
that she is doing better, but you know everything her body
needs, so we ask that you would give it to her. Make her
doctors wise and her family strong. In Jesus' name, amen."

When Mallory finished, everyone was sniffling and
wiping their eyes. There was nothing happy about this
moment, but Mom and I felt loved and grateful for our new
friends. As we left, we knew that God was in control.

When Mom and I arrived back in Dallas, it was late.
Dad was waiting for us at the airport.

He took us directly to the hospital to see Grammy.
When we arrived, she was laying in her long hospital bed
with her eyes closed. There were wires everywhere and
lots of beeping noises. The doctors pulled Mom out of the
room to talk to her privately. "Don't wake her," she told me
before she stepped into the hall.

I stood by Grammy's side and held her hand. It was soft
and warm. She slowly cracked one eye open and curled her
top lip to form a little smile.

I leaned in close, kissed her cheek, and asked why she
was smiling. "Jesus," was all she said. At that moment, I
knew that Grammy was going to be okay. So instead of
being worried or scared for her, I thought about God and
how much He loves us.

A few days later, Grammy came home—back to our
house in Dallas. In my journal I thanked God for taking
care of her.

God,

*Thank you so much for helping Grammy.
I know that You are in control of every
situation that we have, and I know you
were in charge of this one too. But I was
still so scared. I love Grammy so much,
and I never want her to be sick like that.
To be honest, God, I was disappointed to
miss the end of the tour with Mallory, but
Mallory was right, there is nothing more
important than family. And You took care
of that. So anyway, I am glad that Grammy
can come stay with us while she recovers
more. Thank you for taking care of her and
for taking care of everyone who doesn't feel
well. Amen.*

Chapter 15

When it was finally time for the red carpet event—the premiere of *Above the Waters*, my family and I decided it would be easier to get dressed in the hotel Mallory and the Fenways were staying. Even though we weren't far away from the theater, a long black car pulled up to the front of our hotel to take us to the event. It was warm outside, and I was grateful that my blue dress did not have sleeves.

Mr. Fenway warned us that there would be radio stations and news and magazine reporters and photographers hanging out in front of our hotel, as well as at the theater, and he was right. When we pulled up there were people everywhere.

"Lena, over here!" I heard someone call out from across a thick black rope that ran along the sides of the entrance.

I turned my head to the right and looked at the man holding a large black camera.

The bright light flashed before I could smile.

I smiled after and looked away. I hadn't been ready for his picture, and I wanted to ask him to do it again, but it was too late. He had already shifted his camera toward Mallory.

She'd just stepped onto the red carpet behind me, and she looked amazing.

She was wearing a long pink skirt made of layers and layers of a sheer fluffy material. She looked like a walking

136

bowl of cotton candy. Her hair was loosely braided and dangled from the left side of her head. Of course, she was wearing a pair of white cowboy boots with sparkly glitter all over them.

I stopped walking and turned to watch her.

"Lena Daniels!" another voice called out and asked, "How did it feel to act alongside Mallory Winston?"

Before I could answer, I felt Kay B step beside me, gently pulling my arm. "Step forward. This way, Lena." She guided me along the bright red carpet holding a sign that read "Lena Daniels." I was so happy to see Kay B again. I'd missed her and wasn't sure how I managed to get anywhere on time without her. I hadn't seen her since our time on set, and I couldn't wait for a chance to hear about what she'd been up to these last weeks and to fill her in on my touring adventure.

Kay B winked at me and continued to move me forward. "Don't forget to smile!" Kay B whispered in my ear as she stepped away.

Everyone on the other side of the rope seemed to be calling my name while holding out cameras with bright lights attached along with some of the biggest microphones I'd ever seen.

Surprisingly, I didn't feel nervous at all. I didn't have any knots in my stomach and I knew I was right where I was supposed to be. I smiled big and giggled as I inched my way along the carpet.

I felt even more confident when I felt by my dad's arm wrap around my shoulder, followed by my mom's hand on my back, and then three tiny pairs of hands near my waist.

We stood together and smiled until Kay B waved for us to walk forward a little more. At the end of the carpet was the man who'd called out to me earlier. Kay B walked me directly in front of him and said, "Lena, this is Chavis Torry from *Christian Guide*. He can't stay for the entire premiere so he will conduct your interview now."

"Okay." I nodded and looked down at the huge microphone he held out in front of me.

"So, Lena Daniels, tell me what it felt like to star alongside Mallory Winston in *Above the Waters*."

"It was a lot fun." The words, along with a few giggles, escaped my lips.

"Was this your first movie?" he asked.

"Yes . . ." I searched for more words but could not find any.

"Now, I hear there is an interesting story to how you got the part. Tell me a little about it."

"Do you mean how I found out about the audition?"

"Yes. Tell me about that."

"Okay, well, my friend went to a Mallory Winston concert and when she was there she heard about a contest Mallory was having. All you had to do was send Mallory a video telling her about yourself, and she would choose a winner. The winner would have a chance to audition for a part in the movie." I paused and waited for him to finish taking notes on the little pad in his hand.

"Wow, so not only did you win the chance to audition, but you actually got the part!"

I nodded and continued to smile.

"That's awesome! God really opened the door for you

and that's amazing. Was becoming an actress a dream of yours before this?" he asked.

"No, not really," I answered honestly. "But now I realize I really love it."

"Well thank you, Lena Daniels. I look forward to seeing you again up on the big screen."

"Thank you!" I said and turned toward my family. I looked at Kay B for approval before stepping out of the light and trotting off the red carpet.

"Stay close, Daniels family," Kay B instructed. "I need to sneak you past this crowd and get you up on stage quickly to start the night!"

Kay B whizzed us through the crowd, and we found our way to the backstage of the theater. Someone was waiting there for me with a microphone and instructions. Kay B gave Mom and Dad a second to kiss me on the cheek before she told them to follow her.

While I stood there, alone and waiting until it was time to go out on stage, I could hear the excitement in the room. I peeked through a tiny space in the big black curtains and watched as Kay B ushered my family to the front row next to Joey, Emma, and Savannah. I was so glad they could be there to share this event with me. It made everything so much more special.

I put the tiny microphone in my ear like I was told to and waited for the cue.

"Five, four, three, two, and . . ."

I burst through the curtains and waved at the crowd.

"Hi, everyone! My name is Lena Daniels, and I recently acted in the movie, *Above the Waters*! It was a lot of fun.

But, tonight is not about me. It's about God! He is the One who caused all of this amazingness to happen—" The crowd laughed at my new word. I giggled and kept talking until the little voice in my ear told me my time was up. I introduced the next speaker and walked offstage, ready to sit down and enjoy all that was happening around me.

When I took my seat next to my friends and family and stared up at the screen, I wasn't sure what was next for me, but I knew I was ready.

The evening was long and filled with laughter and smiles. After the movie, there was a special reception for the cast and their friends and family. It was so fun seeing everyone again and getting to meet people from their real lives outside of the movie. The more I talked to them, the more I realized that no matter how many movies they had been in or worked on, we were really all alike. Everyone was just happy and grateful for the opportunity. No one seemed famous when they were laughing and relaxing with their families!

One of the hardest parts of the evening was saying goodbye to everyone. None of us knew when or if we would see each other again. Every time I hugged someone, I just smiled and said, "See ya!," because that seemed easier than saying goodbye.

By the time we arrived home, Amber and Ashton were sound asleep in the car. Mom and Dad carried them to their room and tucked them in. Ansley was trying hard to stay awake, but even she was exhausted. She fell asleep as soon as her head landed on her pillow.

I lay with my eyes wide open and waited until I knew

that everyone else was asleep. I wanted to see Grammy. She had come home from the hospital just that morning, and with the excitement and busyness surrounding the red carpet event I had not had time to really talk with her. I hadn't even had time to sit with her and tell her about the tour while she was getting better at the hospital. Mom thought it was a better idea to save the exciting stories until Grammy got out of the hospital and came back to stay with us. I guess that made sense.

I climbed out of bed and walked quietly down the hall to her room. I tapped on the door a few times until I heard her say, "Lena, is that you? Come on in, baby."

Grammy pulled open her covers and held out both of her arms. I climbed in and snuggled up close next to her. "So," she whispered. "I hear you are officially some sort of movie star."

"Grammy! No, I am not." We both chuckled.

"I know you don't think you are a movie star," she said with a more serious voice. "But you are a star. My star—but especially God's star. He is using you to shine His love all over the place!" I just lay next to her quietly relaxing.

"You know, I am so sad that I wasn't able to make it to the event tonight. Tell me all about it!"

I started to feel excited again just thinking about how much fun I'd had. "Grammy, did you see my dress?" I sat up straight in the bed and faced her.

"No! I didn't. Tell me about it!"

"It was blue, and I wore a really pretty silver belt with it!" I described every detail to her, including what color socks and hair bow I wore. Grammy listened carefully.

And once I had finished talking about the premiere, I asked if she wanted to hear about the tour.

"Of course! Tell me everything!" she laughed quietly. I told Grammy every detail that I could remember about the bus and Mr. Ernie. I told her about the live radio interviews and what it was like to stand on a stage in front of thousands of strangers. Of course, when I told her about my "breaking a bone," prayer she laughed so hard that she snorted.

Every time I stopped talking she would say, "What else?!" So I told her more. I told her all about the children's hospital and Caroline and the outfit, the other children at the hospital, and ice cream in the park with my sisters. Then I told her about Austin's chase in the big store and how I helped Ansley with her very own radio interview. We laughed and talked until our faces hurt and our eyes watered.

When I finally finished, I could see that she was tired. I didn't want to stop talking, but I knew she needed her rest. I could tell her about any other details I remembered in the morning. She would be staying with us for a while. So I laid back down in her arms and sighed.

"Good night, Grammy. I love you. I can't wait to see what else God has for me."

"I know He's not finished with you yet, that's for sure. Good night, my little star."

Lena in the Spotlight
Alena Pitts with Wynter Pitts

Hello Stars

Hello Stars introduces Lena Daniels, a Headstrong and determined girl, who has her life planned out to the minute. When Lena unexpectedly lands a movie role, is it too good to be true? This spirited 11-year-old must find a way to balance stardom with "real" life. Suddenly Lena wishes she had time for her three younger sisters and her friends. Find out what happens in *Hello Stars*!

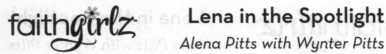

Lena in the Spotlight

Alena Pitts with Wynter Pitts

Shining Night

Lena's overnight fame as an actress con-
tinues to pull her into the spotlight, and
now, she's faced with her biggest chal-
lenge yet. A girl she met at a children's
hospital she visited needs help. To pull
off a concert to raise funds for her new
friend, Lena must take on a huge re-
sponsibility. But as long as Lena remem-
bers that God is her strength and his
plan is bigger, everything will work out.

Available in stores and online!

Connect with Faithgirlz!

  http://www.faithgirlz.com/

www.facebook.com/Faithgirlz/

www.instagram.com/zonderkidz_faithgirlz/

Check out this excerpt from
Book 3 in the Lena in the Spotlight
series: *Shining Night!*

Chapter 1

"Lena! There is a package for you!" Amber was standing in the middle of the kitchen floor staring at me. She was holding a brown box and flashing a toothless grin. After a long day at school I was excited to finally be home. I carefully used my one free hand to push through the door.

I released my lunchbox from my two front teeth and let it fall to the floor. Followed by my backpack, grey sweatshirt, water bottle, and the blue and orange history book that Ms. Blount forced me to bring home. I let out a deep sigh. It felt good to have the use of both my hands and mouth once again.

"Can I open it? Please, please, please?" Amber's grin widened as she begged, teasingly shaking the box right in front of my face.

"Nope!" I leaned forward and pretended I was going grab it out of her hands. Instead I reached both arms out and tickled her belly until she had no choice but to loosen her grip on the box and let me have it.

"Okay, Lena!" She tried to catch her breath as she placed the box in my hands.

I took one look at it and squealed, "It's from Mallory!"

Mom heard the commotion and walked into the kitchen with a curious look on her face. When she saw me holding the box, she smiled.

"Hi, Lena. How was school?" she asked.

"I see you got your package. Did you see that it's from Mallory?" she added.

"I did! I wonder what it is," I said.

"Open it after you get all your things up off the floor!" Mom sneakily grabbed the package from my hands without even giving me a chance to stop her.

My eyes popped open wide with surprise and my mouth dropped. "Mom!" I squealed playfully.

She and Amber exchanged a high-five and giggled.

"Gotcha!"

She was tickled by her ability to move so quickly.

Mom placed the package on the table and headed toward the refrigerator.

"Girls, come get your snack!" she called out for Ansley and Ashton to join us in the kitchen. Normally, after-school snacks are my favorite but today I was much more interested in finding out what was in that box!

I hurried to pick up everything I'd dropped just a few moments ago.

Ansley came running into the kitchen with one arm wrapped tightly around Austin's belly. Austin was wearing a red bandana around his left paw. He looked helpless yet happy with his legs loosely dangling near Ansley's waist. Amber marched behind her wearing her light blue pretend doctor's coat with a white and red plastic stethoscope hanging from her neck. It suddenly made sense. My sisters were playing veterinarian and Austin was, of course, the sick puppy. I smiled.

"Hey, guys."

"Hey, Lena. Did you see your big box?"

"Yup! I'm going to open it in a second."

I rustled Austin's fur a little and tossed my water bottle and entire lunchbox into the sink. *I'll empty it later*, I thought to myself. I grabbed my backpack, sweatshirt, and textbook, and ran them down the hall to my bedroom. I threw it all right on top of my unmade bed and three-day old socks and pajamas. *Ohhh, I should clean up before Mom sees this.* I thought about cleaning it up for a second but decided I didn't want to wait any longer to see what Mallory had sent. I headed back to the kitchen instead.

"Can I open it now, Mom?" I asked, with one hand already tugging at the tape on the side.

Mom nodded and smiled.

Amber, Ashton, Ansley, and even Austin gathered around and waited with excitement as I wrestled with the box until it was finally open enough for us to see a glittery blue box hiding inside.

"It's ... another box!" Amber announced.

Once the blue box was completely free, I could see a tiny white envelope attached to it with three pieces of flowery printed tape. My name was printed in large purple bubble letters across the top.

"It's so cute!" my sisters and I squealed.

Mom peeked over our shoulders and said, "Aww, yes, it is."

"Come on, Lena, open it!" Ansley demanded.

I pulled the card up close to my chest and paused. With four sets of eyes staring at me, and Austin nibbling on my kneecaps, it suddenly felt like maybe I should open the note in private where I could concentrate better.

Mallory had been such a good friend to me. Almost like a big sister. I always took her advice seriously, but I wasn't sure how having to leave the tour with her so suddenly had affected our friendship. When my grandmother got sick, I knew she understood that it was an emergency. But even though she was sympathetic, I still felt bad. She had done so much to make sure that Mom and I and our entire family were comfortable on the road with her. Everything from our own tour bus to the special snacks and treats at each of the venues we appeared. It all seemed like a waste now.

Mom had offered to have me go back once we knew that my grandmother was going to be okay, but Mallory insisted that we stay home and spend time with our family. She'd told me she was really close with her grandmother too, and she understood how scary it could be when they get sick. She even called a few times to pray with us. And when we told her that everything was going to be okay, she cheered, "Thank you, Jesus!" on the other end of the phone.

There was no doubt that she cared about the family, but I had not heard from her since then.

That was at least a month ago.

I couldn't help but wonder why she was reaching out now and not just with a phone call or an email but with a big package.

"Well, Lena. Open it!" Ansley interrupted my thoughts.

I let out a deep breath and opened it.

The notecard was even smaller than the envelope and the front and back were covered in Mallory's handwriting.

"She writes so pretty!" Amber acknowledged.

"She writes a lot," Ashton blurted out.

We all agreed with both.

I stood quietly and read each word on the front side to myself.

When I finished, I could feel the curiosity building in each of my sisters, so I read it again, out loud this time, before flipping to the back.

"Dear Ms. Lena Daniels, ☺

Hey girl! How is life? Sorry I have not been in touch lately, but things have been really busy. I am working on some new music! Can't wait for you to hear it. Well, the tour ended with a great finish. Since you had to leave, we decided to just play a scene from the movie and a little clip from the first interview we did together! That seems like so long ago now. Can you believe how well the movie is going? Mr. Fenway says he thinks we will be nominated for an award! How crazy would that be? Whenever I think about it, I am so grateful that you sent your tape in to audition even if you had red goo stuck on your teeth! I just love how you never let your fears stop you from trying something new. Never stop doing that. Doing something, even when we are afraid, is what it means to have courage. Lena Daniels, you are one courageous girl! God has given you something beautiful to share and I pray you never forget that. Always be willing to tell others about Him. I love thinking about how He showed His love for you during the filming of, *Above the Waters*, on tour as you stood on stage in front of thousands of strangers and at home while you are loving on your grandmother and family!

This is only the beginning for you, my friend!"

I flipped the card over and continued to read.

"I wanted you to know that I'm still praying for your grandmother—that God would continue to give her strength and help her to stay healthy! I want to meet her one day soon!

I also wanted you to know that I miss you so much! I hope this box of goodies makes you smile. I thought carefully about everything I included. I think you will know what they all mean, so I won't explain!

There is one thing that I included that I do want to talk to you about. You'll know when you see it.

We will catch up again soon!

Love, Mallory."

When I finished reading, no one said a word. They were either not impressed with Mallory's note or so curious to see what was actually inside of the mysterious box that they could not think of anything to say.

I think it was the curiosity that kept them quiet because as soon I lifted the top off of the blue box everyone gasped with excitement!

The first thing I spotted was a white sweatshirt, just like the one Mallory was wearing when she visited our family! Ashton held it up high and immediately asked Mom if she could get one.

Right under the sweatshirt was a plastic zipper bag with a pack of gum and a pair of scissors. Mom laughed really hard when she saw this. She remembered our first meeting with Mallory in the airport bathroom as she tried to get that gum out of my hair!

After that I spotted a roll of toilet paper and a pair of black sunglasses. I chuckled. Mallory knew how often I ran to the restroom to cry when I was afraid or nervous, so I assume she wanted me to be well-stocked for whatever my next adventure would be! I guessed the sunglasses were to hide my red eyes.

"Did she send these for us?" Ansley asked while glancing in the box at the four giant-sized packs of fruit snacks attached to a bundle of CDs.

"Yup! I think so!" I said.

Ansley, Ashton, and Amber each grabbed their bundle and immediately asked Mom if they could open them.

Now that we had practically cleared out the box, I could see that there were a few photos lying at the bottom. There was a picture of Mallory and me on stage, another of my mom, dad, and sisters sitting on the tour bus together with our driver, and a few more with friends from the different places we visited. Each one made me smile. Looking at them brought back so many memories of the tour. But the last photo was the one I was least expecting.

There was a picture of Caroline, one of the little girls Mallory and I met when we visited the children's hospital in Tennessee. As soon as I saw it my eyes filled with tears. I could tell this was not just a fun picture to bring back memories. It looked important. I held it up to get a closer look. Attached to the back of the picture was an official looking card with information about Caroline: her birthday, her favorite games to play, and her favorite foods. Below that were the words—*Want to help sponsor me?*

"Mom!" I shouted. "What does this mean?"

Mom took the card and turned it over to read the information.

"Do you know her?" she asked.

"Yes! I met her when Mallory and I visited the children's hospital. Remember I stuffed an outfit in my backpack because I felt like I was supposed to give it to a little girl?"

Mom nodded slowly, remembering.

"That's her! Caroline is the little girl I gave my outfit to. Why does she need a sponsor? Can I do it?"

Mom flipped the card back over and looked up at me with concern in her eyes.

"Well, Lena, it looks like she needs help to pay for the medical treatment she has been getting. The other side of this card with her personal information has more details. Sounds like the hospital has lost funding and is closing. Probably all of the children need help of some sort."

"I want to help her!" I shouted.

"Yeah, let's help her!" Amber agreed.

"Well, girls, medical treatment can be very expensive. Let's talk to Dad when he gets home. We can help her, but I am afraid she may need more than we have to give."

"We have to do something ..." I could feel my eyes filling with tears. "We have to help her."

Mom looked helpless and wrapped her arms around me. Ansley, Amber, and Ashton each wrapped their arms around my waist. We stood quietly for a few more seconds in a group hug.

"We will do something," Mom spoke softly.

Just then Austin announced Dad's arrival with a few loud yelps. He ran to the back door, stood up on his back two legs, and began licking the glass. He dropped down to his belly for a few seconds before jumping up again and repeating this cycle several times until Dad finally walked through the door.

"Dad's home early today!" Amber said with a huge smile. She and Ashton ran to greet him.

Ansley darted towards the kitchen table and grabbed her fruit snacks and CD.

Dad had barely set one foot in the door before Ansley started shouting, "Daddy! Daddy! Look what Mallory sent us!"

"Hey, guys! Aww, is that her newest CD? That's great." Dad's face was bright. He loved all the attention he got when he returned from being gone all day.

"Hi, babe," Mom said while reaching over Austin, Ansley, Amber, and Ashton for a hug.

I waited patiently for my turn.

"Hey, Lena," he said and wrapped an arm around my shoulders. As soon as I laid my head on his chest I could feel the tears starting to come. I wanted to wait to tell him about the hospital, but I couldn't.

"Daddy," I said softly while trying to hold on to my emotions.

"What's going on, Lena? What's wrong?"

Everyone stood still and listened as I retold Dad every detail about meeting Caroline while we were on tour, her sickness, Mallory's box, and my broken heart.

As I talked, Dad's face softened.

"Let's call Mallory. We can get more information on what is happening with the hospital, Caroline, and her family. Then we will see how we can help."

"Can we call now?" I begged.

"Maybe we should wait a little bit. Daddy just walked in," Mom said.

"It's okay. We can try now." Dad gave Mom a little shrug as if to say, Let's get it done so we can eat dinner in peace.

I felt a tiny smile come to my face as Dad pulled out his phone and called Mallory.

He put the phone on speaker and we all stood anxiously as it rang.

Finally we heard Mallory's voice, but it was only her voicemail. After the beep Dad said, "Hi, Mallory, it's the Daniels family. We are all here on speaker ...

"We got your package today. Thank you for all the fun treats. We wanted to talk to you about Caroline and the hospital. Maybe get more details on the situation there. Can you give us a call back when you have a chance?"

Dad finished the call by saying, "Talk to you soon" and hung up.

Ashton looked at me and said, "It's okay, Lena. She'll call back."

I guess she could see the disappointment on my face. I smiled to let her know I appreciated her for trying to cheer me up.

The rest of the evening dragged on. I finished my homework—still no phone call from Mallory. We ate dinner and did our family devotions with still no phone call from Mallory. We took showers and got ready for bed—still no phone call from Mallory.

Mom and Dad called everyone to my room to say goodnight. Dad sat next to me on the edge of the bed and pulled me in close to him. He whispered, "For tonight, all we can do is pray."

CPSIA information can be obtained
at www.ICGtesting.com
Printed in the USA
BVHW032043150523
664226BV00001B/1

9 780310 760634